# John P. Kotter
## on What
## Leaders
## Really
## Do

# John P. Kotter on What Leaders Really Do

John P. Kotter

A HARVARD BUSINESS REVIEW BOOK

**Library of Congress Cataloging-in-Publication Data**

Kotter, John P., 1947–
    John P. Kotter on what leaders really do / John P. Kotter.
        p.      cm.—(A Harvard business review book)
    ISBN 0-87584-897-4 (alk. paper)
    1. Leadership.      I. Title.      II. Series: Harvard business review book
    series.
    HD57.7.K665      1999
    658.4'092—dc21                                                      98-31565
                                                                            CIP

The paper used in this publication meets the requirements of the
American National Standard for Permanence of Paper for Printed Library
Materials Z39.49-1984.

The Michael Richardson story that opens Chapter 7 is from *The General
Managers* by John P. Kotter (pp. 81–85). Copyright © 1982 by The
Free Press. Adapted with permission of The Free Press, a Division of
Simon & Schuster, Inc.

# Contents

# 1

# Leadership at the Turn of the Century

FOR 30 YEARS I have been studying the actions of those
who run organizations, trying to record and clarify what they
do, why they behave as they do, and what effect their choices
have on other individuals and enterprises. I did not begin this
work with an explicit focus on "leadership" in mind—indeed,
the word can be found rarely if at all in my early writings. Nevertheless, it is toward leadership that my efforts have ultimately been
directed, a fact that says something important about the evolv-
ing nature of what we call "managerial" work.

After conducting fourteen formal studies and more than a
thousand interviews, directly observing dozens of executives
in action, and compiling innumerable surveys, I am completely
convinced that most organizations today lack the leadership they
need. And the shortfall is often large. I'm not talking about a
deficit of 10% but of 200%, 400%, or more in positions up and
down the hierarchy. This is not to say that untalented, unener-

---

*Original Introduction, written in 1998.*

1

getic people occupy managerial positions. The typical case is just the opposite, with bright, experienced, and hardworking individuals, some quite extraordinary, almost all trying to do what they believe is right. The problem is that far too few of these people are providing the leadership that is increasingly needed in business, government, everywhere.

Some say that there has been a dearth of quality leadership throughout history. This may or may not be true. What is clear is that the increasingly fast-moving and competitive environment we will face in the twenty-first century demands more leadership from more people to make enterprises prosper. Without that leadership, organizations stagnate, lose their way, and eventually suffer the consequences.

The central issue here is not one of style. I often hear people say that we need a "new leadership style" for the new century. In a globalizing world with a better-educated workforce that is no longer inclined to be seen and not heard, a new leadership style is in fact called for, but style is not the key leadership issue. Substance is. It is about core behavior on the job, not surface detail and tactics, a core that changes little over time, across different cultures, or in different industries.

There are those who say that the consequences of inadequate leadership are minimal because so many factors inside and outside enterprises affect performance. While I would agree in general that many elements contribute to an organization's results, most of these factors can be influenced by good or bad leadership. When that influence points in the wrong direction, in no direction despite rapid change, or along a reasonable trajectory at inadequate speed, the consequences can be tragic. In extreme cases, enterprises fail, jobs are lost, customers and communities and financial interests are hurt, careers are derailed. In less extreme situations, firms underperform, essentially dealing with the same consequences as their ailing counterparts, but to a lesser degree. These failures show up in numbers that are sometimes easy to interpret but are often subtle, as when an enterprise turns out a performance similar to that of its competitors but actually should have done much better, given its assets and starting position.

More dramatic than any numbers are individual cases of real human beings who suffer under tyrants or incompetents or even well-meaning bosses whose failure to lead helps bring down the ship. The pain, broadcast loudly or suffered silently, can be huge, as people lose their jobs to incompetent reengineering or strain under the pressure of propping up a shaky bottom line.

Confront those at the very top of organizations with these facts and many will argue, or at least quietly disagree. "Yes, we could be doing better, but . . ." "Competition forces us to do . . ." "What do you expect in an industry where . . ." This simple confrontational test often separates those executives who understand effective leadership from those who do not.

The leadership gap exists for many reasons, and correcting the problem is made difficult for many additional reasons, not the least being the complexity of the issues. But the problem is not that there is only a limited number of people out there with leadership potential. Even if only one person in a hundred had any potential at all, we would have tens of millions of individuals around the globe providing leadership. This is far from the case today, a fact that should tell us something important about a failure on the part of educational and work organizations, and probably on the part of many families, too.

Instead of nurturing talent, encouraging people to lead and to learn from mistakes and successes, organizations all too often ignore leadership potential, offer no relevant training or role models, and punish those who make small errors while trying to lead. Individuals, too, get in their own way by failing to assess their developmental needs realistically and to proactively seek means of meeting those needs.

The confusion around some of these points occasionally strikes me as staggering. People say "leadership" but describe "management," talk only of a commanding style, serve up speeches about how more than one leader creates chaos, or talk in mystical terms. I have witnessed this cluttered thinking endless times in intelligent people. When capable individuals make such remarks, we have a clear indication of the need for a better understanding of what leaders really do.

## TEN OBSERVATIONS

The body of my work on these subjects has been reported in more than a dozen books and a series of articles. The most important of these articles are six published in the *Harvard Business Review* between 1979 and 1997. These six pieces, along with my integrative commentary, form the mass of this book.

The material collected here deals with the challenges inherent in what is called managerial work and with what differentiates effective from ineffective responses to these challenges. The articles in the first part of the book focus explicitly on leadership and change, that part of organizational activity which I think has become more and more important over the past few decades. Part 2 shows how managerial work today is less about wielding power than about coping with dependence, how managers are put into a far more complex web of interaction with influential others than any organization chart can suggest, and how from these observations important implications follow.

The two parts connect through the notion, much clearer to me now than when I wrote the articles, that more change demands more leadership, which places managers in more complex webs of interaction.

The evolution of these ideas began when I discovered that the most effective people in managerial jobs seemed to act in ways that defied stereotypes of managerial behavior. Later I decided that this "unusual" behavior was mostly related to leadership, which in turn was related to change, one of the central themes of our times.

Reflecting on the six articles now, in 1998, I think hindsight and a bit of finagling put all the big ideas into a set of ten central, interrelated observations. (See Exhibit 1-1.) Each of these observations reflects important changes that continue to occur in the contexts in which managers work, changes driven by powerful forces associated with technology, the globalization of competition and markets, and workforce demographics. These forces have been destroying the mid-twentieth-century stability and pushing up the speed of so much, demanding from managers both incremental change and bigger leaps.

In the mid-twentieth-century world of oligopolies, monopolies, and many barriers to global competition, the longer jumps were not as necessary. Industries changed more slowly, demanding in turn less organizational change. Incremental shifts were for the most part sufficient, perhaps accompanied by a leap every decade or two. In an increasing set of industries today, this behavior is insufficient and can lead to disaster. Thus the number of efforts to transform organizations has increased dramatically in the past few decades, efforts that go by the names of reengineering, restructuring, restrategizing, quality programs, cultural change, and mergers and acquisitions.

EXHIBIT 1-1

## Ten Observations About "Managerial Behavior"

1. When managers produce successful change of any significance in organizations, the effort is usually a time-consuming and highly complex eight-step process, never a one-two-three, hit-and-run affair. Managers who opportunistically skip steps or proceed in the wrong order rarely achieve their aspirations.

2. Although change generally involves a complex, multistage process, regardless of the setting, some essential actions taken by effective managers with transformational goals always vary from case to case to fit key contingencies in their situations. An insensitivity to local contingencies, a one-approach-fits-all attitude, can produce disaster.

3. For a number of reasons, many people influenced by twentieth-century history and the corporate cultures it created—even capable, well-intentioned managers—often make a predictable set of mistakes when attempting to institute significant, nonincremental change.

4. Leadership is different from management, and the primary force behind successful change of any significance is the former, not the latter. Without sufficient leadership, the probability of mistakes increases greatly and the probability of success decreases accordingly. This is true no matter how the change is conceptualized—that is, in terms of new strategies, reengineering, acquisitions, restructuring, quality programs, cultural redesign, and so on.

5. Because the rate of change is increasing, leadership is a growing part of managerial work. Far too many people in positions of power still fail to recognize or acknowledge this most important observation.

6. Increasingly, those in managerial jobs can be usefully thought of as people who create agendas filled with plans (the management part) and visions (the leadership part), as people who develop implementation capacity networks through a well-organized hierarchy (management) and a complex web of aligned relationships (leadership), and who execute through both controls (management) and inspiration (leadership).

7. Because management tends to work through formal hierarchy and leadership does not, as change is breaking down boundaries, creating flatter organizations, more outsourcing, and the demand for more leadership, managerial jobs are placing people in ever more complex webs of relationships.

8. Because managerial work is increasingly a leadership task, and because leaders operate through a complex web of dependent relationships, managerial work is increasingly becoming a game of dependence on others instead of just power over others.

9. When one starts to think of managerial work in terms of networks and dependence, not just hierarchy and formal authority, all sorts of interesting implications follow. Ideas that would have traditionally sounded strange or illegitimate—such as "managing" your boss—suddenly take on importance.

EXHIBIT 1-1

## Continued

10. What a manager / leader does on a minute-by-minute, hour-by-hour basis rarely fits any stereotype of manager, heroic leader, or executive, a fact that can create considerable confusion for those in managerial jobs, especially newcomers. Daily observable behavior is nevertheless understandable if one takes into consideration the diverse tasks (including both leadership and management), the difficult work (including both maintenance and change), and the web of relationships (which goes far beyond formal hierarchy) that come with the territory.

## Observation #1

*When managers today produce successful change of any significance in organizations, regardless of the specific approach, the process is time consuming and highly complex, never a one-two-three, hit-and-run affair.*

In the most successful change efforts, people move through eight complicated stages in which they (1) create a sense of urgency, (2) put together a strong enough team to direct the process, (3) create an appropriate vision, (4) communicate that new vision broadly, (5) empower employees to act on the vision, (6) produce sufficient short-term results to give their efforts credibility and to disempower the cynics, (7) build momentum and use that momentum to tackle the tougher change problems, and (8) anchor the new behavior in organizational culture.

Each of these eight actions associated with successful leaps takes time. Step 1 alone, pushing up the level of urgency, may require many months in a complacent organization of any size. Formulating an appropriate vision and strategies might be done in weeks, but it often requires 12, even 24 months. Creating all the conditions necessary to make a new set of actions stick, not evaporate over time, can take years. These time frames are incomprehensible to short-term, reactive managers. Partially because they are not proactive—indeed, are always trying to catch up with the best competitors—they find the temptation to skip a step or two, or to run through the process too quickly, irresistible. So the reengineering, restructuring, etc., only pushes the organization incrementally, often at great cost.

People do create the appearance of successful change both more quickly and more easily. The big acquisition is made, the structures and systems rationalized, and the process seems to be completed in five months. But appearances deceive. The biggest chore associated with an acquisition of any size is to merge the two (or perhaps more) different cultures. Five months into the process, cultural integration typically has barely begun. Yet if this part of the transformation is ignored or handled poorly, problems will surface for years, maybe decades. Two different ways of operating and two different teams will clash in subtle and obvious ways, diverting attention from the real business of the enterprise.

## Observation #2

*Although change generally involves this complex eight-step process, regardless of the setting, some essential actions taken by effective managers with transformational goals always vary from case to case to fit key contingencies in their situations.*

Differences appropriately arise around the degree to which the vision should be set in stone early on, to which large groups of people should be involved in determining and / or implementing the vision, and to which resistance from various quarters should be heeded.

Many factors affect the choices that need to be made in any specific situation, including the amount of resistance anticipated (the more resistance, the harder it is to push through it); the stakes involved (the bigger the stakes, the more important it is that the vision be right, even if getting it right takes more time and involves many revisions); and the extent to which lower levels in the organization are needed to construct or implement the vision (more dependence on lower levels means allowing them more involvement and participation).

People often get into trouble when they try to apply the tactics that worked in their last change experience without considering how the new situation is different. If, for example, an approach heavy on training has succeeded again and again in helping to empower employees, managers are likely to try it again, even if the central problem is resistance from supervisors and managers, not uneducated subordinates. Or if an approach based on maximum speed has worked well historically, executives continue to charge ahead even though more time is needed to deal with a much more powerful group of resisting employees. In general, the longer a set of tactics has worked, the more oblivious we become to new contingencies. The better a hammer has served in the past, the more all new problems look like nails.

### Observation #3

*For a number of reasons, even very capable and well-intentioned people can make a predictable set of mistakes when they are attempting significant, nonincremental change.*

Failure is associated not only with the untalented. The very capable sometimes allow too much complacency up front. They put together too weak a guiding coalition. They fail to create enough vision, or undercommunicate the vision, or fail to remove sufficient obstacles to change. Their plan to create short-term, credibility-building results is insufficient, they declare victory too soon once initial results are in. They fail to sufficiently connect new approaches to the culture or to create new cultures that can support these approaches. More tactically, they may educate when they need to apply pressure, negotiate over details when better communication is needed, manipulate when being supportive would work much better.

If we all had more experience dealing with major change these errors would occur much less often. But too many people have been trained for and raised in a more stable world, a world that, for the most part, no longer exists. Too many people have been trained only to manage the current system or to make incremental shifts. They have not been shown how to provide the leadership necessary to make bigger leaps.

### Observation #4
*The issue of leadership is centrally important here because leadership is different from management, and the primary force behind successful change is the former, not the latter. Without sufficient leadership, the probability of mistakes increases greatly and the probability of success decreases accordingly.*

Here I'm talking about *leadership* as the development of vision and strategies, the alignment of relevant people behind those strategies, and the empowerment of individuals to make the vision happen, despite obstacles. This stands in contrast with *management,* which involves keeping the current system operating through planning, budgeting, organizing, staffing, controlling, and problem solving. Leadership works through people and culture. It's soft and hot. Management works through hierarchy and systems. It's harder and cooler.

This distinction between management and leadership is neither arbitrary nor semantic. It is, instead, enormously important and a source of great confusion. The person who thinks management is leadership will manage change, hence keeping it under control, but he or she will be unable to provide the stuff required to make larger and more difficult leaps.

Executives who do not lead are almost programmed to fall into all sorts of traps. They rarely push urgency high enough. They underestimate the need for a strong coalition to guide the change. They create only plans and budgets, not the visions and strategies needed to accomplish the vision. They undercommunicate almost any new direction. They fail to eliminate sufficient obstacles so that employees can act on the vision. They declare victory too soon. They do not institutionalize new approaches in organizational culture.

The point here is not that leadership is good and management is bad. They are simply different and serve different purposes. The fundamental purpose of management is to keep the current system functioning. The fundamental purpose of leadership is to produce useful change, especially nonincremental change. It is possible to have too much or too little of either. Strong leadership with no management risks chaos; the organization might walk right off a cliff. Strong management with no leadership tends to entrench an organization in deadly bureaucracy.

**Observation #5**
*Leadership is a growing part of managerial work because the rate of change has been growing.*

A few decades ago a product life cycle might have been 15 years, while today it is 4 for the very same type of product. Thirty years ago, the response time to a customer complaint may have been in days, while now it must be hours. Forty years ago organizations replaced computers within a decade or two, not every 36 months. As a result, effective top executives now might spend up to 80% of their time leading, up from 40% not that long ago. Even those at the bottom of the management hierarchy might spend at least 20% of their time on leadership, and in dynamic industries, even more.

This shift in the nature of "managerial" work is of fundamental importance because leadership and management are so different. It is as if the work needed has suddenly shifted from accounting to accounting and piano playing. Or, for those who play piano at a small restaurant as a second job, it's as if they've been asked to take as their main job membership in a philharmonic orchestra while doing accounting on the side. Under any circumstances, such a shift would be difficult for most people to make and impossible for some. But confusion over what is accounting and what is piano playing would significantly confound the problem.

In a similar way, the confusion over what is leadership and what is management significantly confounds the problem in enterprises today. So people are asked to lead, yet they manage more intensely, becoming frustrated when their actions are not rewarded by superiors or customers. Managers and leaders are not put into teams—one solution to the problem—because the categories are not clear. So managers are teamed with managers. Leaders—what few there are—continue to be seen as potentially dangerous renegades.

Because those helping to run organizations are now being pushed to both manage and lead, the complexity of their position has increased, requiring some new vocabulary.

**Observation #6**
*Increasingly, those in managerial jobs can be usefully thought of as people who create agendas with both plans and budgets (the manage-*

*ment part) and visions and strategies (the leadership part), as people who develop implementation networks both through hierarchy (management) and a complex web of aligned relationships (leadership), and who execute both through controls (management) and inspiration (leadership).*

The proportion of planning versus creating vision, organizing the hierarchy versus aligning the web of relations, controlling versus inspiring, varies with the inclinations of the individual and the demands of the job. Generally, the higher a person goes in an organization, the more he or she needs to be engaged in the work of leadership.

The broad concept of *agendas for action* and *networks of relationships* can be useful when we are talking about managerial behavior because they cut across the categories of leadership and management, thereby providing a degree of unification. Pure managers create agendas and develop networks, as do pure leaders, although the two groups do so in very different ways. But today there are few situations that call for only one or the other; there is usually a need for both types of actions.

The temptation on the part of leadership enthusiasts is to abandon the older vocabulary. But even in jobs demanding much leadership there is typically a managerial component. Agendas and networks can help us evolve from talking only about planning and controls, to talking only about vision and inspiration, to making use of the best of both sets of ideas.

**Observation #7**
*Because management tends to work through formal hierarchy and leadership does not, as change demands more leadership in organizations, managerial jobs are placing people in ever more complex webs of relationships.*

In a more stable world, in which management is the prime activity, jobs of consequence operate through hierarchy. So people look down to their subordinates and up to a boss, as shown on the company organization chart. In a world that is continually changing, where additional leadership is necessary, more individuals outside one's chain of command take on added importance, as do intangibles not on the organization chart, intangibles like corporate culture.

Because a new product strategy may require new information systems, new performance appraisals, new jobs, new attitudes, and more, executives launching the change are forced to concern themselves with many more people than they would in simply pursuing the existing product strategy. Managers fail if they focus only on their subordinates, ignoring for the most part the human resources staff, the information technology (IT) staff, and the layers of other managers who are trying to implement their own visions of change.

**Observation #8**
*Because managerial work is increasingly a leadership task, and because leaders operate through a complex web of dependent relationships, managerial work is increasingly becoming a game of informal dependence on others instead of just formal power over others.*

The wily employee near the bottom of the hierarchy who is seemingly either irrelevant or impotent can make life difficult (or easier) for the "important" manager through any number of strategies. The prototype is Radar in the movie and TV series *M.A.S.H.,* a lowly soldier who could stop a colonel in his tracks. In a world that creates many Radars, an increasing part of managerial work involves actively dealing with dependence on others who are above or below in the hierarchy, peers inside the organization, and even people outside.

The dependence issue is not entirely new. It has been discussed at least since the 1930s, but for the most part quietly and indirectly, at least in serious circles. Less quiet have been tomes on authority, responsibility, span of control, organizational structure, etc., pieces that can be most useful when done well, but which tend to put the spotlight on formal authority, hierarchy, and management. One of my first significant insights as an assistant professor was that because managerial positions make people increasingly dependent on others, including others outside their chain of command, a focus on the dependencies was superior to a traditional emphasis on only formal powers. This idea, which will seem obvious to some, was nevertheless counterintuitive to all who thought of superiors first and foremost as the ones with the power.

Some of my MBA students, especially those with little experience in managerial jobs, find the notion of dependence on others more than confusing. For them managerial work is attractive in the first place because of its attendant perceived power and control. The idea that their prospective careers might push them into jobs of dependence, not just power, is unnerving.

### Observation #9
*When you start to think in terms of networks and dependence and leadership, not just hierarchy and formal authority and management, all sorts of interesting implications follow.*

Giving orders becomes a less important part of the job. Developing good working relationships with people in the network becomes a bigger part of the challenge. Having focus beyond direct subordinates is obviously necessary. Actively managing relations with the boss is a necessity for the good of the enterprise.

This last point struck many as odd when I wrote about it in 1979. With a managerial mindset that looks mostly down the hierarchy, down the chain of command, the concept of managing the boss (MTB) makes little sense outside of a political context. Yet good managers MTB when they have poor bosses to get those superiors to do their managerial tasks well. Also, good leaders always pull everyone relevant along, and the boss is always relevant.

Managing one's superior well, as a part of good management and leadership, especially the latter, means understanding the boss and his or her context, assessing yourself and your needs, and developing and maintaining a relationship that fits both needs and styles, a relationship that is characterized by mutual expectations, that keeps the boss informed, that is based on dependability and honesty, and that makes selective use of the boss's time and resources. This behavior will help you do routine and transformational work, in the latter case helping to avoid the suggestion of being a cowboy. Most organizations put cowboys out to pasture.

### Observation #10

*What a manager / leader does on a minute-by-minute, hour-by-hour basis rarely jibes with any stereotype of a manager, a heroic leader, or an executive, a fact that can create considerable confusion for those new to managerial jobs. This behavior is nevertheless understandable if one takes into consideration the diverse tasks (leadership and management), the difficult work (maintenance and change), and the complex web of relationships (beyond formal hierarchy) that come with the manager's territory.*

A close examination of the day-in, day-out actions and responsibilities of a "manager" or "leader" will produce a picture that
doesn't resemble anything like the "able manager" or "visionary
leader" of our dreams. In "real life," effective executives spend a
lot of time just talking to other people, including people who
are not their subordinates. They deal in a broad sweep of
topics rather than just their functional specialty, are much more
likely to ask questions than to give orders, and actually make
"big" policy decisions only rarely. They engage in the kind of
chitchat and joking that cements relationships. And despite
the fact that they do all of this in a very casual, often disjointed
way, they are remarkably efficient, accomplishing diverse tasks
(that is, the tasks of leadership and of management) in short
periods of time.

If you carefully study effective executives, you can see the
logic of these methods, but the logic is subtle. Because these
tactics have been little studied or taught, relative to other managerial or business subjects, even executives themselves have
difficulty describing what they do and why they do it.

## THOUGHTS AT THE TURN OF THE CENTURY

Reflecting in 1998 on these ten broad observations, along with
more detailed material in the articles, I find myself considering
a number of issues. Today, with more experience, having seen
the long-term effects of many actions, having witnessed spec-
tacular economic results brought about by people with high
moral standards, indeed, having observed the connection between moral standards, leadership, and excellent performance,
I stress a little less MTB and a little more effort to help customers.
I talk a little less about manipulation and a little more about

new product development. Some would say, no doubt, that to serve customers and develop new products one needs to manage the boss and manipulate some situations. I would agree, to a point. But the more frequently these actions are taken without reference to a broader moral framework, the more they are taken without a commitment not to harm others, the greater the chances that tactics for short-term gain will undermine one's capacity to lead over the long term. To some people, this principle will ring true—probably be obvious—but seem of limited significance. From all that I have seen, it is not regarded as anything less than hugely significant to great leaders.

Today there is less confusion about the difference between leadership and management than when I first wrote about it in 1987. But the problem is still monumental. We say leadership when we mean management. We say leadership when we mean some combination of leadership and management. We say leadership when we are talking about people in roles from whom we expect leadership, no matter how these people actually behave. This muddle indicates the general lack of appreciation for what leadership really means.

Without clarity on the meaning of leadership, people fail to develop the right skills. Training focuses on the wrong issues. Sometimes the wrong person is promoted. Most of all, talented people fail to take appropriate actions in their work. They manage change without providing the leadership. They manage people without inspiring them to cope with difficult circumstances. They succeed in keeping the enterprise running but fail to grasp new opportunities or to duck the many new hazards.

The best firms I now know have worked to clarify differences between management and leadership or have been very lucky to have at the helm a great role model for the age we're in. But for most organizations, making this distinction is an ongoing struggle. I've seen a dozen lists of "managerial competencies" in the past few years that are messy conglomerations of management, leadership, and other skills, with items missing and no sense of priorities in light of the context. Intelligent people who care for their enterprises can surely do better.

Clearing up this confusion is important because the topic of change continues to grow in importance. More change demands more leadership, which is difficult to supply if one cannot clearly specify what is the missing element.

Change has always been with us, and always will be. Some thoughtful people see little difference in the rate of evolution today compared with 50 or 100 or 1,000 years ago, but I would disagree. I have seen too many product life cycles cut from 20 to 10 years, or from 5 to 2. I've seen information technology move faster and faster as it affects us all. I've seen events across the globe, which used to affect people slowly, now hit us nearly instantaneously and most influentially. I cannot fathom how this pace will decrease, which has many implications for the topic of leadership.

The current global economic system has about a billion people integrated through products and markets. That's 1 billion out of a total world population of 5.8 billion. Thus, a small town in Germany receives most of its products and services from outside the village. But this integration with the broader economy has not yet been an option for thousands of small towns in India, Iraq, and elsewhere. Almost all futurists predict continuing globalization for a variety of reasons, which means many more people coming into the system, unleashing opportunities and hazards and change. A global system of 2 billion will be even more dynamic than today's 1 billion, and 3 billion will be still more volatile.

Until recently, I have been reluctant to assign a high value to the idea of technology producing significant change. Experts have for so long oversold the impact of technology on our lives that they lost credibility with me. But now we do appear to be moving beyond the industrial age, and the implications are staggering.

One clear indication of the arrival of this technological age is that the biggest consulting firms in the world today are former auditors, and all their work is now IT related. Andersen Consulting alone does billions in business a year, and the number of auditor-consultants seems to be growing at a yearly rate well into double digits. If you had told someone at my college graduation in 1968 that Andersen Consulting would today be nearly ten times bigger than McKinsey, even most techies, I think, would have found the prediction totally without credibility.

One could argue that an increasingly educated workforce is simply a corollary to the new information age. But it has many effects in its own right, at least as these effects influence change and leadership. The person with a third-grade education may see change on the job as threatening. The individual with a master's degree in electrical engineering may want to create change, within certain boundaries. And the latter is less likely to take orders from a manager who knows little about leadership.

In this environment, I now think a twenty-first century, change-ready organization would keep urgency up and complacency down all the time, not just at the beginning of a major change effort. Such an organization would stress teamwork so that it could put together a change-driving coalition on short notice. The enterprise would always have visions at all levels and would update them as appropriate, communicating these ideas widely and constantly. The workforce would always be empowered to run in new directions. And so on. With these characteristics, change that today requires five years might be achieved in one or two, thus helping the firm keep pace with the rapidly changing environment in which it competes.

To cope with all the change and the need for leadership, top managers in the best organizations have been delegating more managerial responsibilities to lower levels. They have also been cleaning house, eliminating activities that are relics from the past. Both actions create space, which gives executives more time to lead. Some of these people find the thought of so much change in their jobs to be threatening, so they resist. Others find the change a blessing, a long-awaited opportunity to have the time to do what they have known for some time was needed.

Firms that are failing to delegate more from the top and to purge unneeded activities are facing increasing burnout among top managers. Fifty-hour weeks go to 60 and then 70 amid growing stress. Decisions stack up in this micromanaged world. Parochial politics often take over as people try to be protective. As a result, organizations can be hurt greatly.

In enterprises that avoid these pitfalls, that delegate more management down from the top, the CEO seems to spend more time on the basic question of purpose. I'm not talking about mission statements but something that can answer questions like: "Why would I want to work here?" "What's the point of what we do?" Without clarity of purpose—and a compelling one at that—well-educated employees can sink easily into a Dilbert-like malaise that is highly dysfunctional.

Further, within enterprises that successfully push appropriate managerial responsibilities down from the top, the middle is usually, though not always, asked to delegate some of its tradi- tional tasks to supervisors and work groups. IT is then used to help the middle better manage the enterprise than the top did in the past. Some middle managers resist the change; they typically claim those beneath them don't have the skills to manage themselves and, if given a chance, will either fail or manage for personal gain. But some in the middle react quite differently. These individuals do not resist. Instead they rejoice, feeling liberated by changes that leave them free to do what they believe is necessary.

If any new sets of responsibilities are to be mastered, even by those who choose not to resist, personal development is typically needed, no matter what a manager's level in the hierarchy. In this regard, good role models can help a great deal. Training sometimes can help. A culture that does not penalize people heavily for making small mistakes definitely helps. This learning is often not easy and rarely comes all at once. But the alternative to growth is destructive to the long-term health of the enterprise as well as to overworked employees.

I'm also struck today with how much people still obsess over changes in the formal trappings of the workplace—organization charts, job descriptions, anything hard and visible and tangible—as a means of creating substantive change. Not that the distribution of formal authority or the arrangement of formal relationships is unimportant. Far from it. But change is more associated with informal networks, while stability goes more with formal hierarchy. Hence, formal roles and relationships are only a part, often a small part, of the terrain during times of transition and transformation. Everyone over 30 and in management knows this truth to some degree, but, faced with difficult challenges, we still often opt for the relatively easy manipulation of boxes and lines.

In many ways, the reengineering revolution has only made this problem worse by using the hard-edged analogy to engineering. So hard is in and soft is out, as has been the case for most of the century, except, possibly, for a decade after *In*

*Search of Excellence* was published in 1982. I think we consultants, sellers of a great deal of reengineering-like work, only exacerbate the problem. Asked to do a project and fast, we too often recommend a reorganization instead of dealing with the more subtle, softer, and difficult behavioral issues. So shift to a global matrix here and put in more IT over there—even though the management can't handle a simpler structure and employees haven't yet absorbed the last round of IT infusion. We rewrite job descriptions when leadership is needed to change behavior.

Rereading the material in the six articles as well as my retrospective commentary, I am once again struck by how difficult managerial jobs can be. Most of these positions require management and at least some leadership. Jobs at the top of the hierarchy, in particular, demand a great deal of leadership to cope with an ever-changing business environment. The people in these jobs must be able to deal with often complex planning systems and controls, organizational structures and staffing systems. They need to live comfortably in large and invisible webs of relationships and to use those relationships to formulate and communicate vision. They need to both inspire and control, seemingly opposite activities.

This reality, in turn, leaves me distressed that so much of our culture does not appreciate the complexity of managerial work and the contributions made to society by those successfully running enterprises. This is not to say that Bill Gates is never held up as a hero. But virtually no one knows what he does, and many think he achieves much for himself and little for society.

The highly influential entertainment industry creates or perpetuates so much misinformation on the subjects in this book as to leave one in distress. Watching dramas and comedies on TV, one would think that a managerial position, especially in a business, is something in which any simpleminded crook could survive and prosper. This may sound like hyperbole, yet I recently read of a study in which the majority of fictional business executives on TV were found to commit crimes. Some of these characters were devious, some fools, but few were dedicated fathers and mothers trying to handle important responsibilities in the service of socially useful goals. It might seem foolish to worry about the influence of such absurdities except that the media is such a powerful propaganda machine.

Meanwhile, K–12 education is even more powerful than TV, despite what some say today about the limits of early education. I have seen little to suggest that this most important social institution, the public or private version, offers much useful information on management. I worry more that the information students do get is tarnished by negative platitudes, such as "managers run businesses only to make as much money as possible." Making money is often thought to conflict with nearly everything worthwhile. Some say business hurts the environment, it hurts people. In this extremist view, executives are practically gangsters, or at least near the bottom of any rational ranking of worthwhile contributors to humankind.

Educators would no doubt object to this characterization, would offer counterexamples of a different and more generous message. Or they might believe that money is so valued in our society that nothing they do will send many students into more useful occupations, such as the arts, government service, or teaching. I would respectfully disagree with both points of view.

I'm certainly not suggesting that we drop fourth-grade art classes for a course in management, but one must wonder if society is well served when doctors and athletes are given high status in K–12 while managers are not. Few youngsters can ultimately get into medical school or the NBA and, increasingly, those who do so work in systems run by managers. In the cases of both the entertainment industry and K–12 education, the effect is to confuse and misdirect, even for young managers and managers to be. In a society that is so dependent on organizations, this surely is not wise.

A final thought. Wisdom is the highest-order aspiration of any article or book; a goal, I fear, that is too seldom met. I think the likelihood of receiving wisdom increases greatly when a person reflects often on his or her own experiences while reading. That is, I hope that you, as a reader of this book, approach it not as a medical text to be absorbed or a menu from which to impulsively pick and choose but as a source of ideas and inspiration that will help you make sense of your past. This method turns reading into serious self-reflection, never an easy task. Yet given the importance of managerial work, this is a task well worth the effort.

# Part 1

# Leadership and Change

# 2

# Choosing Strategies for Change

*John P. Kotter and Leonard A. Schlesinger*

"I T MUST BE CONSIDERED that there is nothing more difficult to carry out, nor more doubtful of success, nor more dangerous to handle, than to initiate a new order of things."[1]

In 1973, The Conference Board asked 13 eminent authorities to speculate what significant management issues and problems would develop over the next 20 years. One of the strongest themes that runs through their subsequent reports is a concern for the ability of organizations to respond to environmental change. As one person wrote:

> It follows that an acceleration in the rate of change will result in an increasing need for reorganization. Reorganization is usually feared, because it means disturbance of

*This article was written with Leonard A. Schlesinger, the George F. Baker, Jr. Professor of Business Administration at the Harvard Business School. The authors wish to thank Vijay Sathe for his help in preparing the article.*
*First published in the March–April 1979* Harvard Business Review.

the status quo, a threat to people's vested interests in their jobs, and an upset to established ways of doing things. For these reasons, needed reorganization is often deferred, with a resulting loss in effectiveness and an increase in costs.[2]

Subsequent events have confirmed the importance of this concern about organizational change. Today, more and more managers must deal with new government regulations, new products, growth, increased competition, technological developments, and a changing work force. In response, most companies or divisions of major corporations find that they must undertake moderate organizational changes at least once a year and major changes every four or five.[3]

Few organizational change efforts tend to be complete failures, but few tend to be entirely successful either. Most efforts encounter problems; they often take longer than expected and desired, they sometimes kill morale, and they often cost a great deal in terms of managerial time or emotional upheaval. More than a few organizations have not even tried to initiate needed changes because the managers involved were afraid that they were simply incapable of successfully implementing them.

In this article, we first describe various causes for resistance to change and then outline a systematic way to select a strategy and set of specific approaches for implementing an organizational change effort. The methods described are based on our analyses of dozens of successful and unsuccessful organizational changes.

## DIAGNOSING RESISTANCE

Organizational change efforts often run into some form of human resistance. Although experienced managers are generally all too aware of this fact, surprisingly few take time before an organizational change to assess systematically who might resist the change initiative and for what reasons. Instead, using past experiences as guidelines, managers all too often apply a simple set of beliefs—such as "engineers will probably resist the change because they are independent and suspicious of top management." This limited approach can create serious problems. Because of the many different ways in which individuals and groups can react to change, correct assessments are often not intuitively obvious and require careful thought.

Of course, all people who are affected by change experience some emotional turmoil. Even changes that appear to be "positive" or "rational" involve loss and uncertainty.[4] Nevertheless, for a number of different reasons, individuals or groups can react very differently to change—from passively resisting it, to aggressively trying to undermine it, to sincerely embracing it.

To predict what form their resistance might take, managers need to be aware of the four most common reasons people resist change. These include: a desire not to lose something of value, a misunderstanding of the change and its implications, a belief that the change does not make sense for the organization, and a low tolerance for change.

## Parochial Self-Interest

One major reason people resist organizational change is that they think they will lose something of value as a result. In these cases, because people focus on their own best interests and not on those of the total organization, resistance often results in "politics" or "political behavior."[5] Consider these two examples:

After a number of years of rapid growth, the president of an organization decided that its size demanded the creation of a new staff function—New Product Planning and Development—to be headed by a vice president. Operationally, this change eliminated most of the decision-making power that the vice presidents of marketing, engineering, and production had over new products. Inasmuch as new products were very important in this organization, the change also reduced the vice presidents' status which, together with power, was very important to them.

During the two months after the president announced his idea for a new product vice president, the existing vice presidents each came up with six or seven reasons the new arrangement might not work. Their objections grew louder and louder until the president shelved the idea.

A manufacturing company had traditionally employed a large group of personnel people as counselors and "father confessors" to its production employees. This group of counselors tended to exhibit high morale because of the professional satisfaction they received from the "helping relationships" they had with employees. When a new performance appraisal system was installed, every six months the counselors were required to provide each employee's supervisor with a written evaluation of the employee's "emotional maturity," "promotional potential," and so forth.

As some of the personnel people immediately recognized, the change would alter their relationships from a peer and helper to more of a boss and evaluator with most of the employees. Predictably, the personnel counselors resisted the change. While publicly arguing that the new system was not as good for the company as the old one, they privately put as much pressure as possible on the personnel vice president until he significantly altered the new system.

Political behavior sometimes emerges before and during organizational change efforts when what is in the best interests of one individual or group is not in the best interests of the total organization or of other individuals and groups.

While political behavior sometimes takes the form of two or more armed camps publicly fighting things out, it usually is much more subtle. In many cases, it occurs completely under the surface of public dialogue. Although scheming and ruthless individuals sometimes initiate power struggles, more often than not those who do are people who view their potential loss from change as an unfair violation of their implicit, or psychological, contract with the organization.[6]

## Misunderstanding and Lack of Trust

People also resist change when they do not understand its implications and perceive that it might cost them much more than they will gain. Such situations often occur when trust is lacking between the person initiating the change and the employees.[7] Here is an example:

When the president of a small midwestern company announced to his managers that the company would implement a flexible working schedule for all employees, it never occurred to him that he might run into resistance. He had been introduced to the concept at a management seminar and decided to use it to make working conditions at his company more attractive, particularly to clerical and plant personnel.

Shortly after the announcement, numerous rumors begin to circulate among plant employees—none of whom really knew what flexible working hours meant and many of whom were distrustful of the manufacturing vice president. One rumor, for instance, suggested that flexible hours meant that most people would have to work whenever their supervisors asked them to—including evenings and weekends. The employee association, a local union, held a quick meeting and then presented the management with a nonnegotiable demand that the flexible hours concept be dropped. The president, caught completely by surprise, complied.

Few organizations can be characterized as having a high level of trust between employees and managers; consequently, it is easy for misunderstandings to develop when change is introduced. Unless managers surface misunderstandings and clarify them rapidly, they can lead to resistance. And that resistance can easily catch change initiators by surprise, especially if they assume that people only resist change when it is not in their best interest.

## Different Assessments

Another common reason people resist organizational change is that they assess the situation differently from their managers or those initiating the change and see more costs than benefits resulting from the change, not only for themselves but for their company as well. For example:

> The president of one moderate-size bank was shocked by his staff's analysis of the bank's real estate investment trust (REIT) loans. This complicated analysis suggested that the bank could easily lose up to $10 million, and that the possible losses were increasing each month by 20%. Within a week, the president drew up a plan to reorganize the part of the bank that managed

REITs. Because of his concern for the bank's stock price, however, he chose not to release the staff report to anyone except the new REIT section manager.

The reorganization immediately ran into massive resistance from the people involved. The group sentiment, as articulated by one person, was: "Has he gone mad? Why in God's name is he tearing apart this section of the bank? His actions have already cost us three very good people [who quit], and have crippled a new program we were implementing [which the president was unaware of] to reduce our loan losses."

Managers who initiate change often assume both that they have all the relevant information required to conduct an adequate organization analysis and that those who will be affected by the change have the same facts, when neither assumption is correct. In either case, the difference in information that groups work with often leads to differences in analyses, which in turn can lead to resistance. Moreover, if the analysis made by those not initiating the change is more accurate than that derived by the initiators, resistance is obviously "good" for the organization. But this likelihood is not obvious to some managers who assume that resistance is always bad and therefore always fight it.[8]

## Low Tolerance for Change

People also resist change because they fear they will not be able to develop the new skills and behavior that will be required of them. All human beings are limited in their ability to change, with some people much more limited than others.[9] Organizational change can inadvertently require people to change too much, too quickly.

Peter F. Drucker has argued that the major obstacle to organizational growth is managers' inability to change their attitudes and behavior as rapidly as their organizations require.[10] Even when managers intellectually understand the need for changes in the way they operate, they sometimes are emotionally unable to make the transition.

It is because of people's limited tolerance for change that individuals will sometimes resist a change even when they realize it is a good one. For example, a person who receives a significantly more important job as a result of an organizational change will probably be very happy. But it is just as possible for such a person to also feel uneasy and to resist giving up certain aspects of the current situation. A new and very different job will require new and different behavior, new and different relationships, as well as the loss of some satisfactory current activities and relationships. If the changes are significant and the individual's tolerance for change is low, he might begin actively to resist the change for reasons even he does not consciously understand.

People also sometimes resist organizational change to save face; to go along with the change would be, they think, an admission that some of their previous decisions or beliefs were wrong. Or they might resist because of peer group pressure or because of a supervisor's attitude. Indeed, there are probably an endless number of reasons why people resist change.[11]

Assessing which of the many possibilities might apply to those who will be affected by a change is important because it can help a manager select an appropriate way to overcome resistance. Without an accurate diagnosis of possibilities of resistance, a manager can easily get bogged down during the change process with very costly problems.

## DEALING WITH RESISTANCE

Many managers underestimate not only the variety of ways people can react to organizational change, but also the ways they can positively influence specific individuals and groups during a change. And, again because of past experiences, managers sometimes do not have an accurate understanding of the advantages and disadvantages of the methods with which they *are* familiar.

### Education and Communication

One of the most common ways to overcome resistance to change is to educate people about it beforehand. Communication of ideas helps people see the need for and the logic of a change. The education process can involve one-on-one discussions, presentations to groups, or memos and reports. For example:

As a part of an effort to make changes in a division's structure and in measurement and reward systems, a division manager put together a one-hour audiovisual presentation that explained the changes and the reasons for them. Over a four-month period, he made this presentation no less than a dozen times to groups of 20 or 30 corporate and division managers.

An education and communication program can be ideal when resistance is based on inadequate or inaccurate information and analysis, especially if the initiators need the resistors' help in implementing the change. But some managers overlook the fact that a program of this sort requires a good relationship between initiators and resistors or that the latter may not believe what they hear. It also requires time and effort, particularly if a lot of people are involved.

## Participation and Involvement

If the initiators involve the potential resistors in some aspect of the design and implementation of the change, they can often forestall resistance. With a participative change effort, the initiators listen to the people the change involves and use their advice. To illustrate:

> The head of a small financial services company once created a task force to help design and implement changes in his company's reward system. The task force was composed of eight second- and third-level managers from different parts of the company. The president's specific charter to them was that they recommend changes in the company's benefit package. They were given six months and asked to file a brief progress report with the president once a month. After they had made their recommendations, which the president largely accepted, they were asked to help the company's personnel director implement them.

We have found that many managers have quite strong feelings about participation—sometimes positive and sometimes negative. That is, some managers feel that there should always be participation during change efforts, while others feel this is virtually always a mistake. Both attitudes can create problems for a manager, because neither is very realistic.

When change initiators believe they do not have all the information they need to design and implement a change, or when they need the wholehearted commitment of others to do so, involving others makes very good sense. Considerable research has demonstrated that, in general, participation leads to commitment, not merely compliance.[12] In some instances, commitment is needed for the change to be a success. Nevertheless, the participation process does have its drawbacks. Not only can it lead to a poor solution if the process is not carefully managed, but also it can be enormously time consuming. When the change must be made immediately, it can take simply too long to involve others.

## Facilitation and Support

Another way that managers can deal with potential resistance to change is by being supportive. This process might include providing training in new skills, or giving employees time off after a demanding period, or simply listening and providing emotional support. For example:

> Management in one rapidly growing electronics company devised a way to help people adjust to frequent organizational changes. First, management staffed its human resource department with four counselors who spent most of their time talking to people who were feeling "burnt out" or who were having difficulty adjusting to new jobs. Second, on a selective basis, management offered people four-week minisabbaticals that involved some reflective or educational activity away from work. And, finally, it spent a great deal of money on in-house education and training programs.

Facilitation and support are most helpful when fear and anxiety lie at the heart of resistance. Seasoned, tough managers often overlook or ignore this kind of resistance, as well as the efficacy of facilitative ways of dealing with it. The basic drawback of this approach is that it can be time consuming and expensive and still fail.[13] If time, money, and patience just are not available, then using supportive methods is not very practical.

## Negotiation and Agreement

Another way to deal with resistance is to offer incentives to active or potential resistors. For instance, management could give a union a higher wage rate in return for a work rule change; it could increase an individual's pension benefits in return for an early retirement. Here is an example of negotiated agreements:

> In a large manufacturing company, the divisions were very interdependent. One division manager wanted to make some major changes in his organization. Yet, because of the interdependence, he recognized that he would be forcing some inconvenience and change on other divisions as well. To prevent top managers in other divisions from undermining his efforts, the division manager negotiated a written agreement with each. The agreement specified the outcomes the other division managers would receive and when, as well as the kinds of cooperation that he would receive from them in return during the change process. Later, whenever the division managers complained about his changes or the change process itself, he could point to the negotiated agreements.

Negotiation is particularly appropriate when it is clear that someone is going to lose out as a result of a change and yet his or her power to resist is significant. Negotiated agreements can be a relatively easy way to avoid major resistance, though, like some other processes, they may become expensive. And once a manager makes it clear that he will negotiate to avoid major resistance, he opens himself up to the possibility of blackmail.[14]

## Manipulation and Co-optation

In some situations, managers also resort to covert attempts to influence others. Manipulation, in this context, normally involves the very selective use of information and the conscious structuring of events.

One common form of manipulation is co-optation. Co-opting an individual usually involves giving him or her a desirable role in the design or implementation of the change. Co-opting a group involves giving one of its leaders, or someone it respects, a key role in the design or implementation of a change. This is not a form of participation, however, because the initiators do not want the advice of the co-opted, merely his or her endorsement. For example:

> One division manager in a large multibusiness corporation invited the corporate human relations vice president, a close friend of the president, to help him and his key staff diagnose some problems the division was having. Because of his busy schedule, the corporate vice president was not able to do much of the actual information gathering or analysis himself, thus limiting his own influence on the diagnoses. But his presence at key meetings helped commit him to the diagnoses as well as the solutions the group designed. The commitment was subsequently very important because the president, at least initially, did not like some of the proposed changes. Nevertheless, after discussion with his human relations vice president, he did not try to block them.

Under certain circumstances co-optation can be a relatively inexpensive and easy way to gain an individual's or a group's support (cheaper, for example, than negotiation and quicker than participation). Nevertheless, it has its drawbacks. If people feel they are being tricked into not resisting, are not being treated equally, or are being lied to, they may respond very negatively. More than one manager has found that, by his effort to give some subordinate a sense of participation through co-optation, he created more resistance than if he had done nothing. In addition, co-optation can create a different kind of problem if those co-opted use their ability to influence the design and implementation of changes in ways that are not in the best interests of the organization.

Other forms of manipulation have drawbacks also, sometimes to an even greater degree. Most people are likely to greet what they perceive as covert treatment and / or lies with a negative response. Furthermore, if a manager develops a reputation as a manipulator, it can undermine his ability to use needed approaches such as education / communication and participation / involvement. At the extreme, it can even ruin his career.

Nevertheless, people do manipulate others successfully—particularly when all other tactics are not feasible or have failed.[15] Having no other alternative, and not enough time to educate, involve, or support people, and without the power or other resources to negotiate, coerce, or co-opt them, managers have resorted to manipulating information channels in order to scare people into thinking there is a crisis coming which they can avoid only by changing.

## Explicit and Implicit Coercion

Finally, managers often deal with resistance coercively. Here they essentially force people to accept a change by explicitly or implicitly threatening them (with the loss of jobs, promotion possibilities, and so forth) or by actually firing or transferring them. As with manipulation, using coercion is a risky process because inevitably people strongly resent forced change. But in situations where speed is essential and where the changes will not be popular, regardless of how they are introduced, coercion may be the manager's only option.

Successful organizational change efforts are always characterized by the skillful application of a number of these approaches, often in very different combinations. However, successful efforts share two characteristics: managers employ the approaches with a sensitivity to their strengths and limitations (see Exhibit 2-1) and appraise the situation realistically.

The most common mistake managers make is to use only one approach or a limited set of them *regardless of the situation*. A surprisingly large number of managers have this problem. This would include the hard-boiled boss who often coerces people, the people-oriented manager who constantly tries to involve and support his people, the cynical boss who always manipulates and co-opts others, the intellectual manager who relies heavily on education and communication, and the lawyerlike manager who usually tries to negotiate.[16]

A second common mistake that managers make is to approach change in a disjointed and incremental way that is not a part of a clearly considered strategy.

## CHOICE OF STRATEGY

In approaching an organizational change situation, managers explicitly or implicitly make strategic choices regarding the speed of the effort, the amount of preplanning, the involvement of others, and the relative emphasis they will give to different

EXHIBIT 2-1

## Methods for Dealing with Resistance to Change

| Approach | Commonly Used in Situations | Advantages | Drawbacks |
|---|---|---|---|
| Education + communication | Where there is a lack of information or inaccurate information and analysis. | Once persuaded, people will often help with the implementation of the change. | Can be very time-consuming if lots of people are involved. |
| Participation + involvement | Where the initiators do not have all the information they need to design the change, and where others have considerable power to resist. | People who participate will be committed to implementing change, and any relevant information they have will be integrated into the change plan. | Can be very time-consuming if participators design an inappropriate change. |
| Facilitation + support | Where people are resisting because of adjustment problems. | No other approach works as well with adjustment problems. | Can be time-consuming, expensive, and still fail. |
| Negotiation + agreement | Where someone or some group will clearly lose out in a change, and where that group has considerable power to resist. | Sometimes it is a relatively easy way to avoid major resistance. | Can be too expensive in many cases if it alerts others to negotiate for compliance. |
| Manipulation + co-optation | Where other tactics will not work, or are too expensive. | It can be a relatively quick and inexpensive solution to resistance problems. | Can lead to future problems if people feel manipulated. |
| Explicit + implicit coercion | Where speed is essential, and the change initiators possess considerable power. | It is speedy, and can overcome any kind of resistance. | Can be risky if it leaves people mad at the initiators. |

EXHIBIT 2-2

## Strategic Continuum

| Fast | Slower |
|------|--------|
| Clearly planned. | Not clearly planned at the beginning. |
| Little involvement of others. | Lots of involvement of others. |
| Attempt to overcome any resistance. | Attempt to minimize any resistance. |

Key situational variables

The amount and type of resistance that is anticipated.

The position of the initiators vis-à-vis the resistors (in terms of power, trust, and so forth).

The locus of relevant data for designing the change, and of needed energy for implementing it.

The stakes involved (e.g., the presence or lack of presence of a crisis, the consequences of resistance and lack of change).

approaches. Successful change efforts seem to be those where these choices both are internally consistent and fit some key situational variables.

The strategic options available to managers can be usefully thought of as existing on a continuum (see Exhibit 2-2).[17] At one end of the continuum, the change strategy calls for a very rapid implementation, a clear plan of action, and little involvement of others. This type of strategy mows over any resistance and, at the extreme, would result in a fait accompli. At the other end of the continuum, the strategy would call for a much slower change process, a less clear plan, and involvement on the part of many people other than the change initiators. This type of strategy is designed to reduce resistance to a minimum.[18]

The further to the left one operates on the continuum in Exhibit 2-2, the more one tends to be coercive and the less one tends to use the other approaches—especially participation; the converse also holds.

Organizational change efforts that are based on inconsistent strategies tend to run into predictable problems. For example, efforts that are not clearly planned in advance and yet are implemented quickly tend to become bogged down owing to unanticipated problems. Efforts that involve a large number of people, but are implemented quickly, usually become either stalled or less participative.

### Situational Factors

Exactly where a change effort should be strategically positioned on the continuum in Exhibit 2-2 depends on four factors:

1. The amount and kind of resistance that is anticipated. All other factors being equal, the greater the anticipated resistance, the more difficult it will be simply to overwhelm it, and the more a manager will need to move toward the right on the continuum to find ways to reduce some of it.[19]

2. The position of the initiator vis-à-vis the resistors, especially with regard to power. The less power the initiator has with respect to others, the more the initiating manager *must* move to the right on the continuum.[20] Conversely, the stronger the initiator's position, the more he or she can move to the left.

3. The person who has the relevant data for designing the change and the energy for implementing it. The more the initiators anticipate that they will need information and commitment from others to help design and implement the change, the more they must move to the right.[21] Gaining useful information and commitment requires time and the involvement of others.

4. The stakes involved. The greater the short-run potential for risks to organizational performance and survival if the present situation is not changed, the more one must move to the left.

Organizational change efforts that ignore these factors inevitably run into problems. A common mistake some managers make, for example, is to move too quickly and involve too few people despite the fact that they do not have all the information they really need to design the change correctly.

Insofar as these factors still leave a manager with some choice of where to operate on the continuum, it is probably best to select a point as far to the right as possible for both economic and social reasons. Forcing change on people can have just too many negative side effects over both the short and the long term. Change efforts using the strategies on the right of the continuum can often help develop an organization and its people in useful ways.[22]

In some cases, however, knowing the four factors may not give a manager a comfortable and obvious choice. Consider a situation where a manager has a weak position vis-à-vis the people whom he thinks need a change and yet is faced with serious consequences if the change is not implemented immediately. Such a manager is clearly in a bind. If he somehow is not able to increase his power in the situation, he will be forced to choose some compromise strategy and to live through difficult times.

## Implications for Managers

A manager can improve his chance of success in an organizational change effort by:

1. Conducting an organizational analysis that identifies the current situation, problems, and the forces that are possible causes of those problems. The analysis should specify the actual importance of the problems, the speed with which the problems must be addressed if additional problems are to be avoided, and the kinds of changes that are generally needed.

2. Conducting an analysis of factors relevant to producing the needed changes. This analysis should focus on questions of who might resist the change, why, and how much, who has information that is needed to design the change, and whose cooperation is essential in implementing it, and what is the position of the initiator vis-à-vis other relevant parties in terms of power, trust, normal modes of interaction, and so forth.

3. Selecting a change strategy, based on the previous analysis, that specifies the speed of change, the amount of preplanning, and the degree of involvement of others; that selects specific tactics for use with various individuals and groups; and that is internally consistent.

4. Monitoring the implementation process. No matter how good a job one does of initially selecting a change strategy

and tactics, something unexpected will eventually occur during implementation. Only by carefully monitoring the process can one identify the unexpected in a timely fashion and react to it intelligently.

Interpersonal skills, of course, are the key to using this analysis. But even the most outstanding interpersonal skills will not make up for a poor choice of strategy and tactics. And in a business world that continues to become more and more dynamic, the consequences of poor implementation choices will become increasingly severe.

# 3

# What Leaders Really Do

L EADERSHIP IS DIFFERENT from management, but not
for the reasons most people think. Leadership isn't mystical
and mysterious. It has nothing to do with having "charisma" or
other exotic personality traits. It is not the province of a chosen
few. Nor is leadership necessarily better than management or a
replacement for it.

Rather, leadership and management are two distinctive and
complementary systems of action. Each has its own function and
characteristic activities. Both are necessary for success in an
increasingly complex and volatile business environment.

Most U.S. corporations today are overmanaged and underled.
They need to develop their capacity to exercise leadership.
Successful corporations don't wait for leaders to come along.
They actively seek out people with leadership potential and expose
them to career experiences designed to develop that potential.

---

*First appeared in the May–June 1990* Harvard Business Review.

Indeed, with careful selection, nurturing, and encouragement, dozens of people can play important leadership roles in a business organization.

But while improving their ability to lead, companies should remember that strong leadership with weak management is no better, and is sometimes actually worse, than the reverse. The real challenge is to combine strong leadership and strong management and use each to balance the other.

Of course, not everyone can be good at both leading and managing. Some people have the capacity to become excellent managers but not strong leaders. Others have great leadership potential but, for a variety of reasons, have great difficulty becoming strong managers. Smart companies value both kinds of people and work hard to make them a part of the team.

But when it comes to preparing people for executive jobs, such companies rightly ignore the recent literature that says people cannot manage *and* lead. They try to develop leader-managers. Once companies understand the fundamental difference between leadership and management, they can begin to groom their top people to provide both.

> *Leadership complements management; it doesn't replace it.*

## THE DIFFERENCE BETWEEN MANAGEMENT AND LEADERSHIP

Management is about coping with complexity. Its practices and procedures are largely a response to one of the most significant developments of the twentieth century: the emergence of large organizations. Without good management, complex enterprises tend to become chaotic in ways that threaten their very existence.

Good management brings a degree of order and consistency to key dimensions like the quality and profitability of products.

Leadership, by contrast, is about coping with change. Part of the reason it has become so important in recent years is that the business world has become more competitive and more volatile. Faster technological change, greater international competition, the deregulation of markets, overcapacity in capital-intensive industries, an unstable oil cartel, raiders with junk bonds, and the changing demographics of the work force are among the many factors that have contributed to this shift. The net result is that doing what was done yesterday, or doing it 5% better, is no longer a formula for success. Major changes are more and more necessary to survive and compete effectively in this new environment. More change always demands more leadership.

Consider a simple military analogy: a peacetime army can usually survive with good administration and management up and down the hierarchy, coupled with good leadership concentrated at the very top. A wartime army, however, needs competent leadership at all levels. No one yet has figured out how to manage people effectively into battle; they must be led.

These different functions—coping with complexity and coping with change—shape the characteristic activities of management and leadership. Each system of action involves deciding what needs to be done, creating networks of people and relationships that can accomplish an agenda, and then trying to ensure that those people actually do the job. But each accomplishes these three tasks in different ways.

Companies manage complexity first by *planning and budgeting*—setting targets or goals for the future (typically for the next month or year), establishing detailed steps for achieving those targets, and then allocating resources to accomplish those plans. By contrast, leading an organization to constructive change begins by *setting a direction*—developing a vision of the future (often the distant future) along with strategies for producing the changes needed to achieve that vision.

Management develops the capacity to achieve its plan by *organizing and staffing*—creating an organizational structure and set of jobs for accomplishing plan requirements, staffing the jobs with qualified individuals, communicating the plan to those people, delegating responsibility for carrying out the plan, and devising systems to monitor implementation. The equivalent leadership activity, however, is *aligning people*. This means communicating the new direction to those who can create coalitions that understand the vision and are committed to its achievement.

Finally, management ensures plan accomplishment by *controlling and problem solving*—monitoring results versus the plan in some detail, both formally and informally, by means of reports, meetings, and other tools; identifying deviations; and then planning and organizing to solve the problems. But for leadership, achieving a vision requires *motivating and inspiring*—keeping people moving in the right direction, despite major obstacles to change, by appealing to basic but often untapped human needs, values, and emotions.

A closer examination of each of these activities will help clarify the skills leaders need.

## SETTING A DIRECTION VS. PLANNING AND BUDGETING

Since the function of leadership is to produce change, setting the direction of that change is fundamental to leadership.

Setting direction is never the same as planning or even long-term planning, although people often confuse the two. Planning is a management process, deductive in nature and designed to produce orderly results, not change. Setting a direction is more inductive. Leaders gather a broad range of data and look for patterns, relationships, and linkages that help explain things. What's more, the direction-setting aspect of leadership does not produce plans; it creates vision and strategies. These describe a business, technology, or corporate culture in terms of what it should become over the long term and articulate a feasible way of achieving this goal. (See "Setting Direction: Lou Gerstner at American Express" at the end of this chapter.)

Most discussions of vision have a tendency to degenerate into the mystical. The implication is that a vision is something mysterious that mere mortals, even talented ones, could never hope to have. But developing good business direction isn't magic. It is a tough, sometimes exhausting process of gathering and analyzing information. People who articulate such visions aren't magicians but broadbased strategic thinkers who are willing to take risks.

Nor do visions and strategies have to be brilliantly innovative; in fact, some of the best are not. Effective business visions regularly have an almost mundane quality, usually consisting of ideas that are already well known. The particular combination or patterning of the ideas may be new, but sometimes even that is not the case.

For example, when CEO Jan Carlzon articulated his vision to make Scandinavian Airline Systems (SAS) the best airline in the world for the frequent business traveler, he was not saying anything that everyone in the airline industry didn't already know. Business travelers fly more consistently than other market segments and are generally willing to pay higher fares. Thus focusing on business customers offers an airline the possibility of high margins, steady business, and considerable growth. But in an industry known more for bureaucracy than vision, no company had ever put these simple ideas together and dedicated itself to implementing them. SAS did, and it worked.

What's crucial about a vision is not its originality but how well it serves the interests of important constituencies— customers, stockholders, employees—and how easily it can be translated into a realistic competitive strategy. Bad visions tend to ignore the legitimate needs and rights of important constituencies—favoring, say, employees over customers or stockholders. Or they are strategically unsound. When a company that has never been better than a weak competitor in an industry suddenly starts talking about becoming number one, that is a pipe dream, not a vision.

One of the most frequent mistakes that overmanaged and underled corporations make is to embrace "long-term planning" as a panacea for their lack of direction and inability to adapt to an increasingly competitive and dynamic business environment. But such an approach misinterprets the nature of direction setting and can never work.

Long-term planning is always time consuming. Whenever something unexpected happens, plans have to be redone. In a dynamic business environment, the unexpected often becomes the norm, and long-term planning can become an extraordinarily burdensome activity. This is why most successful corporations limit the time frame of their planning activities. Indeed, some even consider "long-term planning" a contradiction in terms.

In a company without direction, even short-term planning can become a black hole capable of absorbing an infinite amount of time and energy. With no vision and strategy to provide constraints around the planning process or to guide it, every eventuality deserves a plan. Under these circumstances, contingency planning can go on forever, draining time and attention from far more essential activities, yet without ever providing the clear sense of direction that a company desperately needs. After awhile, managers inevitably become cynical about all this, and the planning process can degenerate into a highly politicized game.

Planning works best not as a substitute for direction setting but as a complement to it. A competent planning process serves as a useful reality check on direction-setting activities. Likewise, a competent direction-setting process provides a focus in which planning can then be realistically carried out. It helps clarify what kind of planning is essential and what kind is irrelevant.

## ALIGNING PEOPLE VS. ORGANIZING AND STAFFING

A central feature of modern organizations is interdependence, where no one has complete autonomy, where most employees are tied to many others by their work, technology, management systems, and hierarchy. These linkages present a special challenge when organizations attempt to change. Unless many individuals line up and move together in the same direction, people will tend to fall all over one another. To executives who are overeducated in management and undereducated in leadership, the idea of getting people moving in the same direction appears to be an organizational problem. What executives need to do, however, is not organize people but align them.

Managers "organize" to create human systems that can implement plans as precisely and efficiently as possible. Typically, this requires a number of potentially complex decisions. A company must choose a structure of jobs and reporting relationships, staff it with individuals suited to the jobs, provide training for those who need it, communicate plans to the work force, and decide how much authority to delegate and to whom. Economic incentives also need to be constructed to accomplish the plan, as well as systems to monitor its implementation. These organizational judgments are much like architectural decisions. It's a question of fit within a particular context.

Aligning is different. It is more of a communications challenge than a design problem. (See "Aligning People: Chuck Trowbridge and Bob Crandall at Eastman Kodak" at the end of this chapter.) First, aligning invariably involves talking to many more individuals than organizing does. The target population can involve not only a manager's subordinates but also bosses, peers, staff in other parts of the organization, as well as suppliers, governmental officials, or even customers. Anyone who can help implement the vision and strategies or who can block implementation is relevant.

Trying to get people to comprehend a vision of an alternative future is also a communications challenge of a completely different magnitude from organizing them to fulfill a short-term plan. It's much like the difference between a football quarterback attempting to describe to his team the next two or three plays versus his trying to explain to them a totally new approach to the game to be used in the second half of the season.

Whether delivered with many words or a few carefully chosen symbols, such messages are not necessarily accepted just because they are understood. Another big challenge in leadership efforts is credibility—getting people to believe the message. Many things contribute to credibility: the track record of the person delivering the message, the content of the message itself, the communicator's reputation for integrity and trustworthiness, and the consistency between words and deeds.

Finally, aligning leads to empowerment in a way that organizing rarely does. One of the reasons some organizations have difficulty adjusting to rapid changes in markets or technology is that so many people in those companies feel relatively powerless. They have learned from experience that even if they correctly perceive important external changes and then initiate appropriate actions, they are vulnerable to someone higher up who does not like what they have done. Reprimands can take many different forms: "That's against policy" or "We can't afford it" or "Shut up and do as you're told."

Alignment helps overcome this problem by empowering people in at least two ways. First, when a clear sense of direction has been communicated throughout an organization, lower level employees can initiate actions without the same degree of vulnerability. As long as their behavior is consistent with the vision, superiors will have more difficulty reprimanding them. Second, because everyone is aiming at the same target, the probability is less that one person's initiative will be stalled when it comes into conflict with someone else's.

## MOTIVATING PEOPLE VS. CONTROLLING AND PROBLEM SOLVING

Since change is the function of leadership, being able to generate highly energized behavior is important for coping with the inevitable barriers to change. Just as direction setting identifies an appropriate path for movement and just as effective alignment gets people moving down that path, successful motivation ensures that they will have the energy to overcome obstacles.

According to the logic of management, control mechanisms compare system behavior with the plan and take action when a deviation is detected. In a well-managed factory, for example, this means the planning process establishes sensible quality targets, the organizing process builds an organization that can achieve those targets, and a control process makes sure that quality lapses are spotted immediately, not in 30 or 60 days, and corrected.

For some of the same reasons that control is so central to management, highly motivated or inspired behavior is almost irrelevant. Managerial processes must be as close as possible to fail-safe and risk-free. That means they cannot be dependent on the unusual or hard to obtain. The whole purpose of systems and structures is to help normal people who behave in normal ways to complete routine jobs successfully, day after day. It's not exciting or glamorous. But that's management.

> *Management controls people by pushing them in the right direction; leadership motivates them by satisfying basic human needs.*

Leadership is different. Achieving grand visions always requires an occasional burst of energy. Motivation and inspiration energize people, not by pushing them in the right direction as control mechanisms do but by satisfying basic human needs for achievement, a sense of belonging, recognition, self-esteem, a feeling of control over one's life, and the ability to live up to one's ideals. Such feelings touch us deeply and elicit a powerful response.

Good leaders motivate people in a variety of ways. First, they always articulate the organization's vision in a manner that stresses the values of the audience they are addressing. This makes the work important to those individuals. Leaders also regularly involve people in deciding how to achieve the organization's vision (or the part most relevant to a particular individual). This gives people a sense of control. Another important motivational technique is to support employee efforts to realize the vision by providing coaching, feedback, and role modeling, thereby helping people grow professionally and enhancing their self-esteem. Finally, good leaders recognize and reward success, which not only gives people a sense of accomplishment but also makes them feel like they belong to an organization that cares about them. When all this is done, the work itself becomes intrinsically motivating.

The more that change characterizes the business environment, the more that leaders must motivate people to provide leadership as well. When this works, it tends to reproduce leadership across the entire organization, with people occupying multiple leadership roles throughout the hierarchy. This is highly valuable, because coping with change in any complex business demands initiatives from a multitude of people. Nothing less will work. (See "Motivating People: Richard Nicolosi at Procter & Gamble" at the end of this chapter.)

Of course, leadership from many sources does not necessarily converge. To the contrary, it can easily conflict. For multiple leadership roles to work together, people's actions must be carefully coordinated by mechanisms that differ from those coordinating traditional management roles.

Strong networks of informal relationships—the kind found in companies with healthy cultures—help coordinate leadership activities in much the same way that formal structure coordinates managerial activities. The key difference is that informal networks can deal with the greater demands for coordination associated with nonroutine activities and change. The multitude of communication channels and the trust among the individuals connected by those channels allow for an ongoing process of accommodation and adaptation. When conflicts arise among roles, those same relationships help resolve the conflicts. Perhaps most important, this process of dialogue and accommodation can produce visions that are linked and compatible instead of remote and competitive. All this requires a great deal more communication than is needed to coordinate managerial roles, but unlike formal structure, strong informal networks can handle it.

Of course, informal relations of some sort exist in all corporations. But too often these networks are either very weak—some people are well connected but most are not—or they are highly fragmented—a strong network exists inside the marketing group and inside R&D but not across the two departments. Such networks do not support multiple leadership initiatives well. In fact, extensive informal networks are so important that if they do not exist, creating them has to be the focus of activity early in a major leadership initiative.

*Despite leadership's growing importance, the on-the-job experiences of most people undermine their ability to lead.*

## CREATING A CULTURE OF LEADERSHIP

Despite the increasing importance of leadership to business success, the on-the-job experiences of most people actually seem to undermine the development of attributes needed for leadership. Nevertheless, some companies have consistently demonstrated an ability to develop people into outstanding leader-managers. Recruiting people with leadership potential is only the first step. Equally important is managing their career patterns. Individuals who are effective in large leadership roles often share a number of career experiences.

Perhaps the most typical and most important is significant challenge early in a career. Leaders almost always have had opportunities during their twenties and thirties to actually try to lead, to take a risk, and to learn from both triumphs and failures. Such learning seems essential in developing a wide range of leadership skills and perspectives. It also teaches people something about both the difficulty of leadership and its potential for producing change.

Later in their careers, something equally important happens that has to do with broadening. People who provide effective leadership in important jobs always have a chance, before they get into those jobs, to grow beyond the narrow base that characterizes most

*One way to develop leadership is to create challenging opportunities for young employees.*

managerial careers. This is usually the result of lateral career moves or of early promotions to unusually broad job assignments. Sometimes other vehicles help, like special task-force assignments or a lengthy general management course. Whatever the case, the breadth of knowledge developed in this way seems to be helpful in all aspects of leadership. So does the network of relationships that is often acquired both inside and outside the company. When enough people get opportunities like this, the relationships that are built also help create the strong informal networks needed to support multiple leadership initiatives.

Corporations that do a better-than-average job of developing leaders put an emphasis on creating challenging opportunities for relatively young employees. In many businesses, decentralization is the key. By definition, it pushes responsibility lower in an organization and in the process creates more challenging jobs at lower levels. Johnson & Johnson, 3M, Hewlett-Packard, General Electric, and many other well-known companies have used that approach quite successfully. Some of those same companies also create as many small units as possible so there are a lot of challenging lower level general management jobs available.

Sometimes these businesses develop additional challenging opportunities by stressing growth through new products or services. Over the years, 3M has had a policy that at least 25% of its revenue should come from products introduced within the last five years. That encourages small new ventures, which in turn offer hundreds of opportunities to test and stretch young people with leadership potential.

Such practices can, almost by themselves, prepare people for small- and medium-sized leadership jobs. But developing people for important leadership positions requires more work on the part of senior executives, often over a long period of time. That work begins with efforts to spot people with great leadership potential early in their careers and to identify what will be needed to stretch and develop them.

Again, there is nothing magic about this process. The methods successful companies use are surprisingly straightforward. They go out of their way to make young employees and people at lower levels in their organizations visible to senior management. Senior managers then judge for themselves who has potential and what the development needs of those people are. Executives also discuss their tentative conclusions among themselves to draw more accurate judgments.

Armed with a clear sense of who has considerable leadership potential and what skills they need to develop, executives in these companies then spend time planning for that development. Sometimes that is done as part of a formal succession planning or high-potential development process; often it is more informal. In either case, the key ingredient appears to be an intelligent assessment of what feasible development opportunities fit each candidate's needs.

To encourage managers to participate in these activities, well-led businesses tend to recognize and reward people who successfully develop leaders. This is rarely done as part of a formal compensation or bonus formula, simply because it is so difficult to measure such achievements with precision. But it does become a factor in decisions about promotion, especially to the most senior levels, and that seems to make a big difference. When told that future promotions will depend to some degree on their ability to nurture leaders, even people who say that leadership cannot be developed somehow find ways to do it.

*Institutionalizing a leadership-centered culture is the ultimate act of leadership.*

Such strategies help create a corporate culture where people value strong leadership and strive to create it. Just as we need more people to provide leadership in the complex organizations that dominate our world today, we also need more people to develop the cultures that will create that leadership. Institutionalizing a leadership-centered culture is the ultimate act of leadership.

## SETTING DIRECTION:
## LOU GERSTNER AT AMERICAN EXPRESS

When Lou Gerstner became president of the Travel Related Services (TRS) arm at American Express in 1979, the unit was facing one of its biggest challenges in AmEx's 130-year history. Hundreds of banks were offering or planning to introduce credit cards through Visa and MasterCard that would compete with the American Express card. And more than two dozen financial service firms were coming into the traveler's checks business. In a mature marketplace, this increase in competition usually reduces margins and prohibits growth.

But that was not how Gerstner saw the business. Before joining American Express, he had spent five years as a consultant to TRS, analyzing the money-losing travel division and the increasingly competitive card operation. Gerstner and his team asked fundamental questions about the economics, market, and competition and developed a deep understanding of the business. In the process, he began to craft a vision of TRS that looked nothing like a 130-year-old company in a mature industry.

Gerstner thought TRS had the potential to become a dynamic and growing enterprise, despite the onslaught of Visa and MasterCard competition from thousands of banks. The key was to focus on the global marketplace and, specifically, on the relatively affluent customer American Express had been traditionally serving with top-of-the-line products. By further segmenting this market, aggressively developing a broad range of new products and services, and investing to increase

CONTINUED

productivity and to lower costs, TRS could provide the best service possible to customers who had enough discretionary income to buy many more services from TRS than they had in the past.

Within a week of his appointment, Gerstner brought together the people running the card organization and questioned all the principles by which they conducted their business. In particular, he challenged two widely shared beliefs—that the division should have only one product, the green card, and that this product was limited in potential for growth and innovation.

Gerstner also moved quickly to develop a more entrepreneurial culture, to hire and train people who would thrive in it, and to clearly communicate to them the overall direction. He and other top managers rewarded intelligent risk taking. To make entrepreneurship easier, they discouraged unnecessary bureaucracy. They also upgraded hiring standards and created the TRS Graduate Management Program, which offered high-potential young people special training, an enriched set of experiences, and an unusual degree of exposure to people in top management. To encourage risk taking among all TRS employees, Gerstner also established something called the Great Performers program to recognize and reward truly exceptional customer service, a central tenet in the organization's vision.

These incentives led quickly to new markets, products, and services. TRS expanded its overseas presence dramatically. By 1988, AmEx cards were issued in 29 currencies (as opposed to only 11 a decade earlier). The unit also focused aggressively on two market segments that had historically received little attention: college students and women. In 1981, TRS

CONTINUED

combined its card and travel-service capabilities to offer corporate clients a unified system to monitor and control travel expenses. And by 1988, AmEx had grown to become the fifth largest direct-mail merchant in the United States.

Other new products and services included 90-day insurance on all purchases made with the AmEx card, a Platinum American Express card, and a revolving credit card known as Optima. In 1988, the company also switched to image-processing technology for billing, producing a more convenient monthly statement for customers and reducing billing costs by 25%.

As a result of these innovations, TRS's net income increased a phenomenal 500% between 1978 and 1987—a compounded annual rate of about 18%. The business outperformed many so-called high-tech / high-growth companies. With a 1988 return on equity of 28%, it also outperformed most low-growth but high-profit businesses.

## ALIGNING PEOPLE: CHUCK TROWBRIDGE AND BOB CRANDALL AT EASTMAN KODAK

Eastman Kodak entered the copy business in the early 1970s, concentrating on technically sophisticated machines that sold, on average, for about $60,000 each. Over the next decade, this business grew to nearly $1 billion in revenues. But costs were high, profits were hard to find, and problems were nearly everywhere. In 1984, Kodak had to write off $40 million in inventory.

CONTINUED

Most people at the company knew there were problems, but they couldn't agree on how to solve them. So, in his first two months as general manager of the new copy products group, established in 1984, Chuck Trowbridge met with nearly every key person inside his group, as well as with people elsewhere at Kodak who could be important to the copier business. An especially crucial area was the engineering and manufacturing organization, headed by Bob Crandall.

Trowbridge and Crandall's vision for engineering and manufacturing was simple: to become a world-class manufacturing operation and to create a less bureaucratic and more decentralized organization. Still, this message was difficult to convey because it was such a radical departure from previous communications, not only in the copy products group but throughout most of Kodak. So Crandall set up dozens of vehicles to emphasize the new direction and align people to it: weekly meetings with his own 12 direct reports; monthly "copy product forums" in which a different employee from each of his departments would meet with him as a group; discuss recent improvements and new projects to achieve still better results; and quarterly "State of the Department" meetings, where his managers met with everybody in their own departments.

Once a month, Crandall and all those who reported to him would also meet with 80 to 100 people from some area of his organization to discuss anything they wanted. To align his biggest supplier—the Kodak Apparatus Division, which supplied one-third of the parts used in design and manufacturing—he and his managers met with the top management of that group over lunch every Thursday. More recently, he has created

CONTINUED

a format called "business meetings," where his managers meet with 12 to 20 people on a specific topic, such as inventory or master scheduling. The goal is to get all of his 1,500 employees in at least one of these focused business meetings each year.

Trowbridge and Crandall also enlisted written communication in their cause. A four- to eight-page "Copy Products Journal" was sent to employees once a month. A program called "Dialog Letters" gave employees the opportunity to anonymously ask questions of Crandall and his top managers and be guaranteed a reply. But the most visible, and powerful, form of written communication was the charts. In a main hallway near the cafeteria, these huge charts vividly reported the quality, cost, and delivery results for each product, measured against difficult targets. A hundred smaller versions of these charts were scattered throughout the manufacturing area, reporting quality levels and costs for specific work groups.

Results of this intensive alignment process began to appear within six months and still more after a year. These successes made the message more credible and helped get more people on board. Between 1984 and 1988, quality on one of the main product lines increased nearly one-hundredfold. Defects per unit went from 30 to 0.3. Over a three-year period, costs on another product line went down nearly 24%. Deliveries on schedule increased from 82% in 1985 to 95% in 1987. Inventory levels dropped by over 50% between 1984 and 1988, even though the volume of products was increasing. And productivity, measured in units per manufacturing employee, more than doubled between 1985 and 1988.

## MOTIVATING PEOPLE: RICHARD NICOLOSI AT PROCTER & GAMBLE

For about 20 years since its founding in 1956, Procter & Gamble's paper products division had experienced little competition for its high-quality, reasonably priced, and well-marketed consumer goods. By the late 1970s, however, the market position of the division had changed. New competitive thrusts hurt P&G badly. For example, industry analysts estimate that the company's market share for disposable diapers fell from 75% in the mid-1970s to 52% in 1984.

That year, Richard Nicolosi came to paper products as the associate general manager, after three years in P&G's smaller and faster moving soft-drink business. He found a heavily bureaucratic and centralized organization that was overly preoccupied with internal functional goals and projects. Almost all information about customers came through highly quantitative market research. The technical people were rewarded for cost savings, the commercial people focused on volume and share, and the two groups were nearly at war with each other.

During the late summer of 1984, top management announced that Nicolosi would become the head of paper products in October, and by August he was unofficially running the division. Immediately he began to stress the need for the division to become more creative and market driven, instead of just trying to be a low-cost producer. "I had to make it very clear," Nicolosi later reported, "that the rules of the game had changed."

CONTINUED

The new direction included a much greater stress on teamwork and multiple leadership roles. Nicolosi pushed a strategy of using groups to manage the division and its specific products. In October, he and his team designated themselves as the paper division "board" and began meeting first monthly and then weekly. In November, they established "category teams" to manage their major brand groups (like diapers, tissues, towels) and started pushing responsibility down to these teams. "Shun the incremental," Nicolosi stressed, "and go for the leap."

In December, Nicolosi selectively involved himself in more detail in certain activities. He met with the advertising agency and got to know key creative people. He asked the marketing manager of diapers to report directly to him, eliminating a layer in the hierarchy. He talked more to the people who were working on new product-development projects.

In January 1985, the board announced a new organizational structure that included not only category teams but also new-brand business teams. By the spring, the board was ready to plan an important motivational event to communicate the new paper products vision to as many people as possible. On June 4, 1985, all the Cincinnati-based personnel in paper plus sales district managers and paper plant managers—several thousand people in all—met in the local Masonic Temple. Nicolosi and other board members described their vision of an organization where "each of us is a leader." The event was videotaped, and an edited version was sent to all sales offices and plants for everyone to see.

All these activities helped create an entrepreneurial environment where large numbers of people were motivated to realize

CONTINUED

the new vision. Most innovations came from people dealing with new products. Ultra Pampers, first introduced in February 1985, took the market share of the entire Pampers product line from 40% to 58% and profitability from break-even to positive. And within only a few months of the introduction of Luvs Delux in May 1987, market share for the overall brand grew by 150%.

Other employee initiatives were oriented more toward a functional area, and some came from the bottom of the hierarchy. In the spring of 1986, a few of the division's secretaries, feeling empowered by the new culture, developed a Secretaries network. This association established subcommittees on training, on rewards and recognition, and on the "secretary of the future." Echoing the sentiments of many of her peers, one paper products secretary said: "I don't see why we too can't contribute to the division's new direction."

By the end of 1988, revenues at the paper products division were up 40% over a four-year period. Profits were up 68%. And this happened despite the fact that the competition continued to get tougher.

# 4

# Leading Change
*Why Transformation Efforts Fail*

O VER THE PAST DECADE, I have watched more than 100 companies try to remake themselves into significantly better competitors. They have included large organizations (Ford) and small ones (Landmark Communications), companies based in the United States (General Motors) and elsewhere (British Airways), corporations that were on their knees (Eastern Airlines), and companies that were earning good money (Bristol-Myers Squibb). These efforts have gone under many banners: total quality management, reengineering, right sizing, restructuring, cultural change, and turnaround. But, in almost every case, the basic goal has been the same: to make fundamental changes in how business is conducted in order to help cope with a new, more challenging market environment.

A few of these corporate change efforts have been very successful. A few have been utter failures. Most fall somewhere in between, with a distinct tilt toward the lower end of the scale.

*First published in the March–April 1995* Harvard Business Review.

The lessons that can be drawn are interesting and will probably be relevant to even more organizations in the increasingly competitive business environment of the coming decade.

The most general lesson to be learned from the more successful cases is that the change process goes through a series of phases that, in total, usually require a considerable length of time. Skipping steps creates only the illusion of speed and never produces a satisfying result. A second very general lesson is that critical mistakes in any of the phases can have a devastating impact, slowing momentum and negating hard-won gains. Perhaps because we have relatively little experience in renewing organizations, even very capable people often make at least one big error.

## ERROR #1:
## NOT ESTABLISHING A GREAT
## ENOUGH SENSE OF URGENCY

Most successful change efforts begin when some individuals or some groups start to look hard at a company's competitive situation, market position, technological trends, and financial performance. They focus on the potential revenue drop when an important patent expires, the five-year trend in declining margins in a core business, or an emerging market that everyone seems to be ignoring. They then find ways to communicate this information broadly and dramatically, especially with respect to crises, potential crises, or great opportunities that are very timely. This first step is essential because just getting a transformation program started requires the aggressive cooperation of many individuals. Without motivation, people won't help and the effort goes nowhere.

Compared with other steps in the change process, phase one can sound easy. It is not. Well over 50% of the companies I have watched fail in this first phase. What are the reasons for that failure? Sometimes executives underestimate how hard it can be to drive people out of their comfort zones. Sometimes they grossly overestimate how successful they have already been in increasing urgency. Sometimes they lack patience: "Enough with the preliminaries; let's get on with it." In many cases, executives become paralyzed by the downside possibilities. They worry that employees with seniority will become defensive, that morale will drop, that events will spin out of control, that short-term business results will be jeopardized, that the stock will sink, and that they will be blamed for creating a crisis.

A paralyzed senior management often comes from having too many managers and not enough leaders. Management's mandate is to minimize risk and to keep the current system operating. Change, by definition, requires creating a new system, which in turn always demands leadership. Phase one in a renewal process typically goes nowhere until enough real leaders are promoted or hired into senior-level jobs.

Transformations often begin, and begin well, when an organization has a new head who is a good leader and who sees the need for a major change. If the renewal target is the entire company, the CEO is key. If change is needed in a division, the division general manager is key. When these individuals are not new leaders, great leaders, or change champions, phase one can be a huge challenge.

Bad business results are both a blessing and a curse in the first phase. On the positive side, losing money does catch people's attention. But it also gives less maneuvering room. With good business results, the opposite is true: convincing people of the need for change is much harder, but you have more resources to help make changes.

But whether the starting point is good performance or bad, in the more successful cases I have witnessed, an individual or a group always facilitates a frank discussion of potentially unpleasant facts: about new competition, shrinking margins, decreasing market share, flat earnings, a lack of revenue growth, or other relevant indices of a declining competitive position. Because there seems to be an almost universal human tendency to shoot the bearer of bad news, especially if the head of the organization is not a change champion, executives in these companies often rely on outsiders to bring unwanted information. Wall Street analysts, customers, and consultants can all be helpful in this regard. The purpose of all this activity, in the words of one former CEO of a large European company, is "to make the status quo seem more dangerous than launching into the unknown."

> *One chief executive officer deliberately engineered the largest accounting loss in the history of the company.*

In a few of the most successful cases, a group has manufactured a crisis. One CEO deliberately engineered the largest accounting loss in the company's history, creating huge pressures from Wall Street in the process. One division president commissioned first-ever customer-satisfaction surveys, knowing full well that the results would be terrible. He then made these findings public. On the surface, such moves can look unduly risky. But there is also risk in playing it too safe: when the urgency rate is not pumped up enough, the transformation process cannot succeed and the long-term future of the organization is put in jeopardy.

When is the urgency rate high enough? From what I have seen, the answer is when about 75% of a company's management is honestly convinced that business-as-usual is totally unacceptable. Anything less can produce very serious problems later on in the process.

## ERROR #2:
## NOT CREATING A POWERFUL
## ENOUGH GUIDING COALITION

Major renewal programs often start with just one or two people. In cases of successful transformation efforts, the leadership coalition grows and grows over time. But whenever some minimum mass is not achieved early in the effort, nothing much worthwhile happens.

It is often said that major change is impossible unless the head of the organization is an active supporter. What I am talking about goes far beyond that. In successful transformations, the chairman or president or division general manager, plus another 5 or 15 or 50 people, come together and develop a shared commitment to excellent performance through renewal. In my experience, this group never includes all of the company's most senior executives because some people just won't buy in, at least not at first. But in the most successful cases, the coalition is always pretty powerful—in terms of titles, information and expertise, reputations and relationships.

In both small and large organizations, a successful guiding team may consist of only three to five people during the first year of a renewal effort. But in big companies, the coalition needs to grow to the 20 to 50 range before much progress can be made in phase three and beyond. Senior managers always form the core of the group. But sometimes you find board members, a representative from a key customer, or even a powerful union leader.

Because the guiding coalition includes members who are not part of senior management, it tends to operate outside of the normal hierarchy by definition. This can be awkward, but it is clearly necessary. If the existing hierarchy were working well, there would be no need for a major transformation. But since the current system is not working, reform generally demands activity outside of formal boundaries, expectations, and protocol.

A high sense of urgency within the managerial ranks helps enormously in putting a guiding coalition together. But more is usually required. Someone needs to get these people together, help them develop a shared assessment of their company's problems and opportunities, and create a minimum level of trust and communication.

*In failed transformations, you often find plenty of plans and programs, but no vision.* Off-site retreats, for two or three days, are one popular vehicle for accomplishing this task. I have seen many groups of 5 to 35 executives attend a series of these retreats over a period of months.

Companies that fail in phase two usually underestimate the difficulties of producing change and thus the importance of a powerful guiding coalition. Sometimes they have no history of teamwork at the top and therefore undervalue the importance of this type of coalition. Sometimes they expect the team to be led by a staff executive from human resources, quality, or strategic planning instead of a key line manager. No matter how capable or dedicated the staff head, groups without strong line leadership never achieve the power that is required.

Efforts that don't have a powerful enough guiding coalition can make apparent progress for a while. But, sooner or later, the opposition gathers itself together and stops the change.

## ERROR #3:
## LACKING A VISION

In every successful transformation effort that I have seen, the guiding coalition develops a picture of the future that is relatively easy to communicate and appeals to customers, stockholders, and employees. A vision always goes beyond the numbers that are typically found in five-year plans. A vision says something that helps clarify the direction in which an organization needs to move. Sometimes the first draft comes mostly from a single individual. It is usually a bit blurry, at least initially. But after the coalition works at it for 3 or 5 or even 12 months, something much better emerges through their tough analytical thinking and a little dreaming. Eventually, a strategy for achieving that vision is also developed.

In one midsize European company, the first pass at a vision contained two-thirds of the basic ideas that were in the final product. The concept of global reach was in the initial version from the beginning. So was the idea of becoming preeminent in certain businesses. But one central idea in the final version— getting out of low value-added activities—came only after a series of discussions over a period of several months.

Without a sensible vision, a transformation effort can easily dissolve into a list of confusing and incompatible projects that can take the organization in the wrong direction or nowhere at all. Without a sound vision, the reengineering project in the accounting department, the new 360-degree performance appraisal from the human resources department, the plant's quality program, the cultural change project in the sales force will not add up in a meaningful way.

In failed transformations, you often find plenty of plans and directives and programs, but no vision. In one case, a company gave out four-inch-thick notebooks describing its change effort. In mind-numbing detail, the books spelled out procedures, goals, methods, and deadlines. But nowhere was there a clear and compelling statement of where all this was leading. Not surprisingly, most of the employees with whom I talked were either confused or alienated. The big, thick books did not rally them together or inspire change. In fact, they probably had just the opposite effect.

In a few of the less successful cases that I have seen, management had a sense of direction, but it was too complicated or blurry to be useful. Recently, I asked an executive in a midsize company to describe his vision and received in return a barely comprehensible 30-minute lecture. Buried in his answer were the basic elements of a sound vision. But they were buried—deeply.

*A vision says something that clarifies the direction in which an organization needs to move.*

A useful rule of thumb: if you can't communicate the vision to someone in five minutes or less and get a reaction that signifies both understanding and interest, you are not yet done with this phase of the transformation process.

## ERROR #4:
## UNDERCOMMUNICATING THE
## VISION BY A FACTOR OF TEN

I've seen three patterns with respect to communication, all very common. In the first, a group actually does develop a pretty good transformation vision and then proceeds to communicate it by holding a single meeting or sending out a single communication. Having used about .0001% of the yearly intracompany communication, the group is startled that few people seem to understand the new approach. In the second pattern, the head of the organization spends a considerable amount of time making speeches to employee groups, but most people still don't get it (not surprising, since vision captures only .0005% of the total yearly communication). In the third pattern, much more effort goes into newsletters and speeches, but some very visible senior executives still behave in ways that are antithetical to the vision. The net result is that cynicism among the troops goes up, while belief in the communication goes down.

Transformation is impossible unless hundreds or thousands of people are willing to help, often to the point of making short-term sacrifices. Employees will not make sacrifices, even if they are unhappy with the status quo, unless they believe that useful change is possible. Without credible communication, and a lot of it, the hearts and minds of the troops are never captured.

This fourth phase is particularly challenging if the short-term sacrifices include job losses. Gaining understanding and support is tough when downsizing is a part of the vision. For this reason, successful visions usually include new growth possibilities and the commitment to treat fairly anyone who is laid off.

Executives who communicate well incorporate messages into their hour-by-hour activities. In a routine discussion about a business problem, they talk about how proposed solutions fit (or don't fit) into the bigger picture. In a regular performance appraisal, they talk about how the employee's behavior helps or undermines the vision. In a review of a division's quarterly performance, they talk not only about the numbers but also about how the division's executives are contributing to the transformation. In a routine Q&A with employees at a company facility, they tie their answers back to renewal goals.

In more successful transformation efforts, executives use all existing communication channels to broadcast the vision. They turn boring and unread company newsletters into lively articles about the vision. They take ritualistic and tedious quarterly management meetings and turn them into exciting discussions of the transformation. They throw out much of the company's generic management education and replace it with courses that focus on business problems and the new vision. The guiding principle is simple: use every possible channel, especially those that are being wasted on nonessential information.

Perhaps even more important, most of the executives I have known in successful cases of major change learn to "walk the talk." They consciously attempt to become a living symbol of the new corporate culture. This is often not easy. A 60-year-old plant manager who has spent precious little time over 40 years thinking about customers will not suddenly behave in a customer-oriented way. But I have witnessed just such a person change, and change a great deal. In that case, a high level of urgency helped. The fact that the man was a part of the guiding coalition and the vision-creation team also helped. So did all the communication, which kept reminding him of the desired behavior, and all the feedback from his peers and subordinates, which helped him see when he was not engaging in that behavior.

*Too often, an employee understands the new vision and wants to help make it happen. But something appears to be blocking the path.*

Communication comes in both words and deeds, and the latter are often the most powerful form. Nothing undermines change more than behavior by important individuals that is inconsistent with their words.

## ERROR #5:
## NOT REMOVING OBSTACLES TO
## THE NEW VISION

Successful transformations begin to involve large numbers of people as the process progresses. Employees are emboldened to try new approaches, to develop new ideas, and to provide leadership. The only constraint is that the actions fit within the broad parameters of the overall vision. The more people involved, the better the outcome.

To some degree, a guiding coalition empowers others to take action simply by successfully communicating the new direction. But communication is never sufficient by itself. Renewal also requires the removal of obstacles. Too often, an employee understands the new vision and wants to help

*Worst of all are bosses who refuse to change and who make demands that are inconsistent with the overall effort.*

make it happen. But an elephant appears to be blocking the path. In some cases, the elephant is in the person's head, and the challenge is to convince the individual that no external obstacle exists. But in most cases, the blockers are very real.

Sometimes the obstacle is the organizational structure: narrow job categories can seriously undermine efforts to increase productivity or make it very difficult even to think about customers. Sometimes compensation or performance-appraisal systems make people choose between the new vision and their own self-interest. Perhaps worst of all are bosses who refuse to change and who make demands that are inconsistent with the overall effort.

One company began its transformation process with much publicity and actually made good progress through the fourth phase. Then the change effort ground to a halt because the officer in charge of the company's largest division was allowed to undermine most of the new initiatives. He paid lip service to the process but did not change his behavior or encourage his managers to change. He did not reward the unconventional ideas called for in the vision. He allowed human resource systems to remain intact even when they were clearly inconsistent with the new ideals. I think the officer's motives were complex. To some degree, he did not believe the company needed major change. To some degree, he felt personally threatened by all the change. To some degree, he was afraid that he could not produce both change and the expected operating profit. But despite the fact that they backed the renewal effort, the other officers did virtually nothing to stop the one blocker. Again, the reasons were complex. The company had no history of confronting problems like this. Some people were afraid of the officer. The CEO was concerned that he might lose a talented executive. The net result was disastrous. Lower level managers concluded that senior management had lied to them about their commitment to renewal, cynicism grew, and the whole effort collapsed.

In the first half of a transformation, no organization has the momentum, power, or time to get rid of all obstacles. But the big ones must be confronted and removed. If the blocker is a person, it is important that he or she be treated fairly and in a way that is consistent with the new vision. But action is essential, both to empower others and to maintain the credibility of the change effort as a whole.

## ERROR #6:
## NOT SYSTEMATICALLY
## PLANNING FOR AND CREATING
## SHORT-TERM WINS

Real transformation takes time, and a renewal effort risks losing momentum if there are no short-term goals to meet and celebrate. Most people won't go on the long march unless they see compelling evidence within 12 to 24 months that the journey is producing expected results. Without short-term wins, too many people give up or actively join the ranks of those people who have been resisting change.

One to two years into a successful transformation effort, you find quality beginning to go up on certain indices or the decline in net income stopping. You find some successful new product introductions or an upward shift in market share. You find an impressive productivity improvement or a statistically higher customer-satisfaction rating. But whatever the case, the win is unambiguous. The result is not just a judgment call that can be discounted by those opposing change.

Creating short-term wins is different from hoping for short-term wins. The latter is passive, the former active. In a successful transformation, managers actively look for ways to obtain clear performance improvements, establish goals in the yearly planning system, achieve the objectives, and reward the people involved with recognition, promotions, and even money. For example, the guiding coalition at a U.S. manufacturing company produced a highly visible and successful new product introduction about 20 months after the start of its renewal effort. The new product was selected about six months into the effort because it met multiple criteria: it could be designed and launched in a relatively short period; it could be handled by a small team of people who were devoted to the new vision; it had upside potential; and the new product-development team could operate outside the established departmental structure without practical problems. Little was left to chance, and the win boosted the credibility of the renewal process.

Managers often complain about being forced to produce short-term wins, but I've found that pressure can be a useful element in a change effort. When it becomes clear to people that major change will take a long time, urgency levels can drop. Commitments to produce short-term wins help keep the urgency level up and force detailed analytical thinking that can clarify or revise visions.

*While celebrating a win is fine, declaring the war won can be catastrophic.*

## ERROR #7:
## DECLARING VICTORY TOO SOON

After a few years of hard work, managers may be tempted to declare victory with the first clear performance improvement. While celebrating a win is fine, declaring the war won can be catastrophic. Until changes sink deeply into a company's culture, a process that can take five to ten years, new approaches are fragile and subject to regression.

In the recent past, I have watched a dozen change efforts operate under the reengineering theme. In all but two cases, victory was declared and the expensive consultants were paid and thanked when the first major project was completed after two to three years. Within two more years, the useful changes that had been introduced slowly disappeared. In two of the ten cases, it's hard to find any trace of the reengineering work today.

Over the past 20 years, I've seen the same sort of thing happen to huge quality projects, organizational development efforts, and more. Typically, the problems start early in the process: the urgency level is not intense enough, the guiding coalition is not powerful enough, and the vision is not clear enough. But it is the premature victory celebration that kills momentum. And then the powerful forces associated with tradition take over.

Ironically, it is often a combination of change initiators and change resistors that creates the premature victory celebration. In their enthusiasm over a clear sign of progress, the initiators go overboard. They are then joined by resistors, who are quick to spot any opportunity to stop change. After the celebration is over, the resistors point to the victory as a sign that the war has been won and the troops should be sent home. Weary troops allow themselves to be convinced that they won. Once home, the foot soldiers are reluctant to climb back on the ships. Soon thereafter, change comes to a halt, and tradition creeps back in.

Instead of declaring victory, leaders of successful efforts use the credibility afforded by short-term wins to tackle even bigger problems. They go after systems and structures that are not consistent with the transformation vision and have not been confronted before. They pay great attention to who is promoted, who is hired, and how people are developed. They include new reengineering projects that are even bigger in scope than the initial ones. They understand that renewal efforts take not months but years. In fact, in one of the most successful transformations that I have ever seen, we quantified the amount of change that occurred each year over a seven-year period. On a scale of one (low) to ten (high), year one received a two, year two a four, year three a three, year four a seven, year five an eight, year six a four, and year seven a two. The peak came in year five, fully 36 months after the first set of visible wins.

## ERROR #8:
## NOT ANCHORING CHANGES IN
## THE CORPORATION'S CULTURE

In the final analysis, change sticks when it becomes "the way we do things around here," when it seeps into the bloodstream of the corporate body. Until new behaviors are rooted in social norms and shared values, they are subject to degradation as soon as the pressure for change is removed.

Two factors are particularly important in institutionalizing change in corporate culture. The first is a conscious attempt to show people how the new approaches, behaviors, and attitudes have helped improve performance. When people are left on their own to make the connections, they sometimes create very inaccurate links. For example, because results improved while charismatic Harry was boss, the troops link his mostly idiosyncratic style with those results instead of seeing how their own improved customer service and productivity were instrumental. Helping people see the right connections requires communication. Indeed, one company was relentless, and it paid off enormously. Time was spent at every major management meeting to discuss why performance was increasing. The company newspaper ran article after article showing how changes had boosted earnings.

The second factor is taking sufficient time to make sure that the next generation of top management really does personify the new approach. If the requirements for promotion don't change, renewal rarely lasts. One bad succession decision at the top of an organization can undermine a decade of hard work. Poor succession decisions are possible when boards of directors are not an integral part of the renewal effort. In at least three instances I have seen, the champion for change was the retiring executive, and although his successor was not a resistor, he was not a change champion. Because the boards did not understand the transformations in any detail, they could not see that their choices were not good fits. The retiring executive in one case tried unsuccessfully to talk his board into a less seasoned candidate who better personified the transformation. In the other two cases, the CEOs did not resist the boards' choices, because they felt the transformation could not be undone by their successors. They were wrong. Within two years, signs of renewal began to disappear at both companies.

There are still more mistakes that people make, but these eight are the big ones (see Exhibit 4-1). I realize that in a short article everything is made to sound a bit too simplistic. In reality, even successful change efforts are messy and full of surprises. But just as a relatively simple vision is needed to guide people through a major change, so a vision of the change process can reduce the error rate. And fewer errors can spell the difference between success and failure.

EXHIBIT 4-1

## Eight Steps to Transforming Your Organization

**Establishing a Sense of Urgency**                                       1
Examining market and competitive realities
Identifying and discussing crises, potential crises, or major opportunities

↓

**Forming a Powerful Guiding Coalition**                                  2
Assembling a group with enough power to lead the change effort
Encouraging the group to work together as a team

↓

**Creating a Vision**                                                     3
Creating a vision to help direct the change effort
Developing strategies for achieving that vision

↓

**Communicating the Vision**                                             4
Using every vehicle possible to communicate the new vision and strategies
Teaching new behaviors by the example of the guiding coalition

↓

**Empowering Others to Act on the Vision**                               5
Getting rid of obstacles to change
Changing systems or structures that seriously undermine the vision
Encouraging risk taking and nontraditional ideas, activities, and actions

↓

**Planning for and Creating Short-Term Wins**                            6
Planning for visible performance improvements
Creating those improvements
Recognizing and rewarding employees involved in the improvements

↓

**Consolidating Improvements and Producing Still More Change**           7
Using increased credibility to change systems, structures, and policies that
    don't fit the vision
Hiring, promoting, and developing employees who can implement the vision
Reinvigorating the process with new projects, themes, and change agents

↓

**Institutionalizing New Approaches**                                    8
Articulating the connections between the new behaviors and corporate success
Developing the means to ensure leadership development and succession

# Part 2

# Dependency and Networks

# 5

# Power, Dependence, and Effective Management

A MERICANS, AS A RULE, are not very comfortable with power or with its dynamics. We often distrust and question the motives of people who we think actively seek power. We have a certain fear of being manipulated. Even those people who think the dynamics of power are inevitable and needed often feel somewhat guilty when they themselves mobilize and use power. Simply put, the overall attitude and feeling toward power, which can easily be traced to the nation's very birth, is negative. In his enormously popular *Greening of America*, Charles Reich reflects the views of many when he writes, "It is not the misuse of power that is evil; the very existence of power is evil."[1]

*Author's note: This reading is based on data from a clinical study of a highly diverse group of 26 organizations including large and small, public and private, manufacturing and service organizations. The study was funded by the Division of Research at the Harvard Business School. As part of the study process, the author interviewed about 250 managers. First published in the July–August 1977* Harvard Business Review.

One of the many consequences of this attitude is that power as a topic for rational study and dialogue has not received much attention, even in managerial circles. If the reader doubts this, all he or she need do is flip through some textbooks, journals, or advanced management course descriptions. The word *power* rarely appears.

This lack of attention to the subject of power merely adds to the already enormous confusion and misunderstanding surrounding the topic of power and management. And this misunderstanding is becoming increasingly burdensome because in today's large and complex organizations the effective performance of most managerial jobs requires one to be skilled at the acquisition and use of power.

From my own observations, I suspect that a large number of managers—especially the young, well-educated ones—perform significantly below their potential because they do not understand the dynamics of power and because they have not nurtured and developed the instincts needed to effectively acquire and use power.

In this reading I hope to clear up some of the confusion regarding power and managerial work by providing tentative answers to three questions:

1. Why are the dynamics of power necessarily an important part of managerial processes?
2. How do effective managers acquire power?
3. How and for what purposes do effective managers use power?

I will not address questions related to the misuse of power, but not because I think they are unimportant. The fact that some managers, some of the time, acquire and use power mostly for their own aggrandizement is obviously a very important issue that deserves attention and careful study. But that is a complex topic unto itself and one that has already received more attention than the subject of this article.

## RECOGNIZING DEPENDENCE
## IN THE MANAGER'S JOB

One of the distinguishing characteristics of typical managers is how dependent they are on the activities of a variety of other people to perform their jobs effectively.[2] Unlike doctors and mathematicians, whose performance is more directly dependent on their own talents and efforts, a manager can be dependent in varying degrees on superiors, subordinates, peers in other parts of the organization, the subordinates of peers, outside suppliers, customers, competitors, unions, regulating agencies, and many others.

These dependency relationships are an inherent part of managerial jobs because of two organizational facts of life: division of labor and limited resources. Because the work in organizations is divided into specialized divisions, departments, and jobs, managers are made directly or indirectly dependent on many others for information, staff services, and cooperation in general. Because of their organizations' limited resources, managers are also dependent on their external environments for support. Without some minimal cooperation from suppliers, competitors, unions, regulatory agencies, and customers, managers cannot help their organizations survive and achieve their objectives.

Dealing with these dependencies and the manager's subsequent vulnerability is an important and difficult part of a manager's job because, while it is theoretically possible that all of these people and organizations would automatically act in just the manner that a manager wants and needs, such is almost never the case in reality. All the people on whom a manager is dependent have limited time, energy, and talent, for which there are competing demands.

Some people may be uncooperative because they are too busy elsewhere, and some because they are not really capable of helping. Others may well have goals, values, and beliefs that are quite different and in conflict with the manager's and may therefore have no desire whatsoever to help or cooperate. This is obviously true of a competing company and sometimes of a union, but it can also apply to a boss who is feeling threatened by a manager's career progress or to a peer whose objectives clash with the manager's.

Indeed, managers often find themselves dependent on many people (and things) whom they do not directly control and who are not cooperating. This is the key to one of the biggest frustrations managers feel in their jobs, even in the top ones, which the following example illustrates:

After nearly a year of rumors, it was finally announced that the president of ABC Corporation had been elected chairman of the board and that Jim Franklin, the vice president of finance, would replace him as president. While everyone at ABC was aware that a shift would take place soon, it was not at all clear before the announcement who would be the next president. Most people had guessed it would be Phil Cook, the marketing vice president.

Nine months into his job as chief executive officer, Franklin found that Phil Cook (still the marketing vice president) seemed to be fighting him in small and subtle ways. There was never anything blatant, but Cook just did not cooperate with Franklin as the other vice presidents did. Shortly after being elected, Franklin had tried to bypass what he saw as a potential conflict with Cook by telling him that he would understand if Cook would prefer to move somewhere else where he could be a CEO also. Franklin said that it would be a big loss to the company but that he would be willing to help Cook in a number of ways if he wanted to look for a presidential opportunity elsewhere. Cook had thanked him but had said that family and community commitments would prevent him from relocating and all CEO opportunities were bound to be in a different city.

Since the situation did not improve after the tenth and eleventh months, Franklin seriously considered forcing Cook out. When he thought about the consequences of such a move, Franklin became more and more aware of just how dependent he was on Cook. Marketing and sales were generally the keys to success in their industry, and the company's sales force was one of the best, if not the best, in the industry. Cook had been with the company for 25 years. He had built a strong personal relationship with many of the people in the sales force and was universally popular. A mass exodus just might occur if Cook were fired. The loss of a large number of salespeople, or even a lot of turmoil in the department, could have a serious effect on the company's performance.

After one year as chief executive officer, Franklin found that the situation between Cook and himself had not improved and had become a constant source of frustration.

As a person gains more formal authority in an organization, the areas in which he or she is vulnerable increase and become more complex rather than the reverse. As the previous example suggests, it is not at all unusual for the president of an organization to be in a highly dependent position, a fact often not apparent to either the outsider or to the lower-level manager who covets the president's job.

A considerable amount of the behavior of highly successful managers that seems inexplicable in light of what management texts usually tell us managers do becomes understandable when one considers a manager's need for, and efforts at, managing his or her relationships with others.[3] To be able to plan, organize, budget, staff, control, and evaluate, managers need some control over the many people on whom they are dependent. Trying to control others solely by directing them and on the basis of the power associated with one's position simply will not work—first, because managers are always dependent on some people over whom they have no formal authority, and second, because virtually no one in modern organizations will passively accept and completely obey a constant stream of orders from someone just because he or she is the "boss."

Trying to influence others by means of persuasion alone will not work either. Although it is very powerful and possibly the single most important method of influence, persuasion has some serious drawbacks too. To make it work requires time (often lots of it), skill, and information on the part of the persuader. And persuasion can fail simply because the other person chooses not to listen or does not listen carefully.

This is not to say that directing people on the basis of the formal power of one's position and persuasion are not important means by which successful managers cope. They obviously are. But, even taken together, they are not usually enough.

Successful managers cope with their dependence on others by being sensitive to it, by eliminating or avoiding unnecessary dependence and by establishing power over those others. Good managers then use that power to help them plan, organize, staff, budget, evaluate, and so on. *In other words, it is primarily because of the dependence inherent in managerial jobs that the dynamics of power necessarily form an important part of a manager's processes.*

An argument that took place during a middle-management training seminar I participated in a few years ago helps illustrate further this important relationship between a manager's need for power and the degree of his or her dependence on others:

Two participants, both managers in their thirties, got into a heated disagreement regarding the acquisition and use of power by managers. One took the position that power was absolutely central to managerial work, while the other argued that it was virtually irrelevant. In support of their positions, each described a very "successful" manager with whom he worked. In one of these examples, the manager seemed to be constantly developing and using power, while in the other, such behavior was rare. Subsequently, both seminar participants were asked to describe their successful managers' jobs in terms of the dependence *inherent* in those jobs.

The young manager who felt power was unimportant described a staff vice president in a small company who was dependent only on his immediate subordinates, his peers, and his boss. This person, Joe Phillips, had to depend on his subordinates to do their jobs appropriately, but, if necessary, he could fill in for any of them or secure replacement for them rather easily. He also had considerable formal authority over them; that is, he could give them raises and new assignments, recommend promotions, and fire them. He was moderately dependent on the other four vice presidents in the company for information and cooperation. They were likewise dependent on him. The president had considerable formal authority over Phillips but was also moderately dependent on him for help, expert advice, the service his staff performed, other information, and general cooperation.

The second young manager—the one who felt power was very important—described a service department manager, Sam Weller, in a large, complex, and growing company who was in quite a different position. Weller was dependent not only on his boss for rewards and information, but also on 30 other individuals who made up the divisional and corporate top management. And while his boss, like Phillips's, was moderately dependent on him too, most of the top managers were not. Because Weller's subordinates, unlike Phillips's, had people reporting to them, Weller was dependent not only on his subordinates but also on his subordinates' subordinates. Because he could not himself easily replace or do most of their technical jobs, unlike Phillips, he was very dependent on all these people.

In addition, for critical supplies, Weller was dependent on two other department managers in the division. Without their timely help, it was impossible for his department to do its job. These departments, however, did not have similar needs for Weller's help and cooperation. Weller was also dependent on local labor union officials and on a federal agency that regulated the division's industry. Both could shut his division down if they wanted.

Finally, Weller was dependent on two outside suppliers of key materials. Because of the volume of his department's purchase relative to the size of these two companies, he had little power over them.

Under these circumstances, it is hardly surprising that Sam Weller had to spend considerable time and effort acquiring and using power to manage his many dependencies, while Joe Phillips did not.

As this example also illustrates, not all management jobs require an incumbent to be able to provide the same amount of successful power-oriented behavior. But most management jobs today are more like Weller's than Phillips's. And, perhaps more important, the trend over the past two or three decades is away from jobs like Phillips's and toward jobs like Weller's. So long as our technologies continue to become more complex, the average organization continues to grow larger, and the average industry continues to become more competitive and regulated, that trend will continue; as it does so, the effective acquisition and use of power by managers will become even more important.

## ESTABLISHING POWER IN RELATIONSHIPS

To help cope with the dependency relationships inherent in their jobs, effective managers create, increase, or maintain four different types of power over others.[4] Having power based in these areas puts the manager in a position both to influence those people on whom he or she is dependent when necessary and to avoid being hurt by any of them.

### Sense of Obligation

One of the ways that successful managers generate power in their relationships with others is to create a sense of obligation in those others. When the manager is successful, the others feel that they should—rightly—allow the manager to influence them within certain limits.

Successful managers often go out of their way to do favors for people who they expect will feel an obligation to return those favors. As can be seen in the following description of a manager by one of his subordinates, some people are very skilled at identifying opportunities for doing favors that cost them very little but that others appreciate very much:

> Most of the people here would walk over hot coals in their bare feet if my boss asked them to. He has an incredible capacity to do little things that mean a lot to people. Today, for example, in his junk mail he came across an advertisement for something that one of my subordinates had in passing once mentioned that he was shopping for. So my boss routed it to him. That probably took 15 seconds of his time, and yet my subordinate really appreciated it. To give you another example, two weeks ago he somehow learned that the purchasing manager's mother had died. On his way home that night, he stopped off at the funeral parlor. Our purchasing manager was, of course, there at the time. I bet he'll remember that brief visit for quite a while.

Recognizing that most people believe that friendship carries with it certain obligations ("A friend in need . . ."), successful managers often try to develop true friendships with those on whom they are dependent. They will also make formal and informal deals in which they give something up in exchange for certain future obligations.

## Belief in a Manager's Expertise

A second way successful managers gain power is by building reputations as "experts" in certain matters. Believing in the manager's expertise, others will often defer to the manager on those matters. Managers usually establish this type of power through visible achievement. The larger the achievement and the more visible it is, the more power the manager tends to develop.

One of the reasons that managers display concern about their "professional reputations" and their track records is that these have an impact on others' beliefs about their expertise. These factors become particularly important in large settings, where most people have only secondhand information about most other people's professional competence, as the following shows:

> Herb Randley and Bert Kline were both 35-year-old vice presidents in a large research and development organization. According to their closest associates, they were equally bright and competent in their technical fields and as managers. Yet Randley had a much stronger professional reputation in most parts of the company, and his ideas generally carried much more weight. Close friends and associates claim the reason that Randley is so much more powerful is related to a number of tactics that he has used more than Kline has.
>
> Randley has published more scientific papers and managerial articles than Kline. Randley has been more selective in the assignments he has worked on, choosing those that are visible and that require his strong suits. He has given more speeches and presentations on projects that are his own achievements. And in meetings in general, he is allegedly forceful in areas where he has expertise and silent in those where he does not.

### Identification with a Manager

A third method by which managers gain power is by fostering others' unconscious identification with them or with ideas they stand for. Sigmund Freud was the first to describe this phenomenon, which is most clearly seen in the way people look up to charismatic leaders. Generally, the more a person finds a manager both consciously and (more important) unconsciously an ideal person, the more he or she will defer to that manager.

Managers develop power based on others' idealized views of them in a number of ways. They try to look and behave in ways that others respect. They go out of their way to be visible to their employees and to give speeches about their organizational goals, values, and ideals. They even consider, while making hiring and promotion decisions, whether they will be able to develop this type of power over the candidates:

> One vice president of sales in a moderate-sized manufacturing company was reputed to be so much in control of his sales force that he could get them to respond to new and different marketing programs in a third of the time taken by the company's best competitors. His power over his employees was based primarily on their strong identification with him and what he stood for. Emigrating to the United States at age 17, this person worked his way up "from nothing." When made a sales manager in 1965, he began recruiting other young immigrants and sons of immigrants from his former country. When made vice president of sales in 1970, he continued to do so. In 1975, 85% of his sales force was made up of people whom he hired directly or who were hired by others he brought in.

## Perceived Dependence
## on a Manager

The final way that an effective manager often gains power is by feeding others' beliefs that they are dependent on the manager either for help or for not being hurt. The more they perceive they are dependent, the more most people will be inclined to cooperate with such a manager.

There are two methods that successful managers often use to create perceived dependence.

### Finding and Acquiring Resources

In the first, the manager identifies and secures (if necessary) resources that another person requires to perform the job, resources that he or she does not possess, and that are not readily available elsewhere. These resources include such things as authority to make certain decisions; control of money, equipment, and office space; access to important people; information and control of information channels; and subordinates. Then the manager takes action so that the other person correctly perceives that the manager has such resources and is willing and ready to use them to help (or hinder) the other person. Consider the following extreme—but true—example.

> When young Tim Babcock was put in charge of a division of a large manufacturing company and told to "turn it around," he spent the first few weeks studying it from afar. He decided that the division was in disastrous shape and that he would need to take many large steps quickly to save it. To be able to do that, he realized he needed to develop considerable power fast over most of the division's management and staff. He did the following:
>
> 1. He gave the division's management two hours' notice of his arrival.
> 2. He arrived in a limousine with six assistants.
> 3. He immediately called a meeting of the 40 top managers.

4. He outlined briefly his assessment of the situation, his commitment to turn things around, and the basic direction he wanted things to move in.

5. He then fired the four top managers in the room and told them that they had to be out of the building in two hours.

6. He then said he would personally dedicate himself to sabotaging the career of anyone who tried to block his efforts to save the division.

7. He ended the 60-minute meeting by announcing that his assistants would set up appointments for him with each of them starting at 7:00 the next morning.

Throughout the critical six-month period that followed, those who remained at the division generally cooperated energetically with Mr. Babcock.

### Affecting Perceptions of Resources

A second way effective managers gain these types of power is by influencing other persons' perceptions of the manager's resources.[5] In settings where many people are involved and where the manager does not interact continuously with those he or she is dependent on, those people will seldom possess hard facts regarding what relevant resources the manager commands directly or indirectly (through others), what resources he or she will command in the future, or how prepared he or she is to use those resources to help or hinder them. They will be forced to make their own judgments.

Insofar as managers can influence people's judgments, they can generate much more power than one would generally ascribe to them in light of the reality of their resources.

In trying to influence people's judgments, managers pay considerable attention to the "trappings" of power and to their own reputations and images. Among other actions, they sometimes carefully select, decorate, and arrange their offices in ways that give signs of power. They associate with people or organizations that are known to be powerful or that others perceive as powerful. Managers selectively foster rumors concerning their own power. Indeed, those who are particularly skilled at creating power in this way tend to be very sensitive to the impressions that all their actions might have on others.

## Formal Authority

Before discussing how managers use their power to influence others, it is useful to see how formal authority relates to power. By *formal authority*, I mean those elements that automatically come with a managerial job—perhaps a title, an office, a budget, the right to make certain decisions, a set of subordinates, a reporting relationship, and so on.

Effective managers use the elements of formal authority as resources to help them develop any or all of the four types of power previously discussed, just as they use other resources (such as their education). Two managers with the same formal authority can have very different amounts of power entirely because of the way they have used that authority. For example:

1. By sitting down with employees who are new or with people who are starting new projects and clearly specifying who has the formal authority to do what, one manager creates a strong sense of obligation in others to defer to her authority later.

2. By selectively withholding or giving the high-quality service his department can provide other departments, one manager makes other managers clearly perceive that they are dependent on him.

On its own, then, formal authority does not guarantee a certain amount of power; it is only a resource that managers can use to generate power in their relationships.

## EXERCISING POWER TO INFLUENCE OTHERS

Successful managers use the power they develop in their relationships, along with persuasion, to influence people on whom they are dependent to behave in ways that make it possible for the managers to get their jobs done effectively. They use their power to influence others directly, face to face, and in more indirect ways. (See Exhibit 5-1.)

### Face-to-Face Influence

The chief advantage of influencing others directly by exercising any of the types of power is speed. If the power exists and the manager correctly understands the nature and strength of it, he or she can influence the other person with nothing more than a brief request or command:

Jones thinks Smith feels obliged to him for past favors. Furthermore, Jones thinks that his request to speed up a project by two days probably falls within a zone that Smith would consider legitimate in light of his own definition of his obligation to Jones.

EXHIBIT 5-1

# Methods of Influence

| Face-to-face Methods | What They Can Influence | Advantages | Drawbacks |
|---|---|---|---|
| Exercise obligation-based power. | Behavior within zone that the other perceives as legitimate in light of the obligation. | Quick. Requires no outlay of tangible resources. | If the request is outside the acceptable zone, it will fail; if it is too far outside, others might see it as illegitimate. |
| Exercise power based on perceived expertise. | Attitudes and behavior within the zone of perceived expertise. | Quick. Requires no outlay of tangible resources. | If the request is outside the acceptable zone, it will fail; if it is too far outside, others might see it as illegitimate. |
| Exercise power based on identification with a manager. | Attitudes and behavior that are not in conflict with the ideals that underlie the identification. | Quick. Requires no expenditure of limited resources. | Restricted to influence attempts that are not in conflict with the ideals that underlie the identification. |
| Exercise power based on perceived dependence. | Wide range of behavior that can be monitored. | Quick. Can often succeed when other methods fail. | Repeated influence attempts encourage the other to gain power over the influencer. |
| Coercively exercise power based on perceived dependence. | Wide range of behavior that can be easily monitored. | Quick. Can often succeed when other methods fail. | Invites retaliation. Very risky. |
| Use persuasion. | Very wide range of attitudes and behavior. | Can produce internalized motivation that does not require monitoring. Requires no power or outlay of scarce material resources. | Can be very time-consuming. Requires other person to listen. |

**EXHIBIT 5-1**

## Continued

| Face-to-face Methods | What They Can Influence | Advantages | Drawbacks |
| --- | --- | --- | --- |
| Combine these methods. | Depends on the exact combination. | Can be more potent and less risky than using a single method. | More costly than using a single method. |

| Indirect Methods | What They Can Influence | Advantages | Drawbacks |
| --- | --- | --- | --- |
| Manipulate the other's environment by using any or all of the face-to-face methods. | Wide range of behavior and attitudes. | Can succeed when face-to-face methods fail. | Can be time-consuming. Is complex to implement. Is very risky, especially if used frequently. |
| Change the forces that continuously act on the individual: Formal organizational arrangements. Informal social arrangements. Technology. Resources available. Statement of organizational goals. | Wide range of behavior and attitudes on a continuous basis. | Has continuous influence, not just a one-shot effect. Can have a very powerful impact. | Often requires a considerable power outlay to achieve. |

So Jones simply calls Smith and makes his request. Smith pauses for only a second and says yes, he'll do it.

Manager Johnson has some power based on perceived dependence over manager Baker. When Johnson tells Baker that he wants a report done in 24 hours, Baker grudgingly considers the costs of compliance, of noncompliance, and of complaining to higher authorities. He decides that doing the report is the least costly action and tells Johnson he will do it.

Porter identifies strongly with Marquette, an older manager who is not her boss. Porter thinks Marquette is the epitome of a great manager and tries to model herself after her. When Marquette asks Porter to work on a special project "that could be very valuable in improving the company's ability to meet new competitive products," Porter agrees without hesitation and works 15 hours per week above and beyond her normal hours to get the project done and done well.

When used to influence others, each of the four types of power has different advantages and drawbacks. For example, power based on perceived expertise or on identification with a manager can often be used to influence attitudes as well as someone's immediate behavior and thus can have a lasting impact. It is very difficult to influence attitudes by using power based on perceived dependence, but if it can be done, it usually has the advantage of being able to influence a much broader range of behavior than the other methods do. When exercising power based on perceived expertise, for example, one can only influence attitudes and behavior within that narrow zone defined by the expertise.

The drawbacks associated with the use of power based on perceived dependence are particularly important to recognize. A person who feels dependent on a manager for rewards (or lack of punishments) might quickly agree to a request from the manager but then not follow through—especially if the manager cannot easily find out if the person has obeyed or not. Repeated influence attempts based on perceived dependence also seem to encourage the other person to try to gain some power to balance the manager's. And perhaps most important, using power based on perceived dependence in a coercive way is very risky. Coercion invites retaliation.

For instance, in the example in which Tim Babcock took such extreme steps to save the division he was assigned to "turn around," his development and use of power based on perceived dependence could have led to mass resignation and the collapse of the division. Babcock fully recognized this risk, however, and behaved as he did because he felt there was simply *no other way* that he could gain the very large amount of quick cooperation needed to save the division.

Effective managers will often draw on more than one form of power to influence someone, or they will combine power with persuasion. In general, they do so because a combination can be more potent and less risky than any single method, as the following description shows:

> One of the best managers we have in the company has lots of power based on one thing or another over most people. But he seldom if ever just tells or asks someone to do something. He almost always takes a few minutes to try to persuade them. The power he has over people generally induces them to listen carefully and certainly disposes them to be influenced. That, of course, makes the persuasion process go quickly and easily. And he never risks getting the other person mad or upset by making what that person thinks is an unfair request or command.

It is also common for managers not to coercively exercise power based on perceived dependence by itself, but to combine it with other methods to reduce the risk of retaliation. In this way, managers are able to have a large impact without leaving the bitter aftertaste of punishment alone.

## Indirect Influence Methods

Effective managers also rely on two types of less direct methods to influence those on whom they are dependent. In the first way, they use any or all of the face-to-face methods to influence other people, who in turn have some specific impact on a desired person.

Product manager Stein needed plant manager Billings to "sign off" on a new product idea (Product X) which Billings thought was terrible. Stein decided that there was no way he could logically persuade Billings because Billings just would not listen to him. With time, Stein felt, he could have broken through that barrier. But he did not have that time. Stein also realized that Billings would never, just because of some deal or favor, sign off on a product he did not believe in. Stein also felt it not worth the risk of trying to force Billings to sign off, so here is what he did:

> On Monday, Stein got Reynolds, a person Billings respected, to send Billings two market research studies that were very favorable to Product X, with a note attached saying, "Have you seen this? I found them rather surprising. I am not sure if I entirely believe them, but still. . . ."

> On Tuesday, Stein got a representative of one of the company's biggest customers to mention casually to Billings on the phone that he had heard a rumor about Product X being introduced soon and was "glad to see you guys are on your toes as usual."

On Wednesday, Stein had two industrial engineers stand about three feet away from Billings as they were waiting for a meeting to begin and talk about the favorable test results on Product X.

On Thursday, Stein set up a meeting to talk about Product X with Billings and invited only people whom Billings liked or respected and who also felt favorably about Product X.

On Friday, Stein went to see Billings and asked him if he was willing to sign off on Product X. He was.

This type of manipulation of the environments of others can influence both behavior and attitudes and can often succeed when other influence methods fail. But it has a number of serious drawbacks. It takes considerable time and energy, and it is quite risky. Many people think it is wrong to try to influence others in this way, even people who, without consciously recognizing it, use this technique themselves. If they think someone is trying, or has tried, to manipulate them, they may retaliate. Furthermore, people who gain the reputation of being manipulators seriously undermine their own capacities for developing power and for influencing others. Almost no one, for example, will want to identify with a manipulator. And virtually no one accepts, at face value, a manipulator's sincere attempts at persuasion. In extreme cases, a reputation as a manipulator can completely ruin a manager's career.

A second way in which managers indirectly influence others is by making permanent changes in an individual's or a group's environment. They change job descriptions, the formal systems that measure performance, the extrinsic incentives available, the tools, people, and other resources that the people or groups work with, the architecture, the norms or values of work groups, and so on. If the manager is successful in making the changes, and the changes have the desired effect on the individual or group, that effect will be sustained over time.

Effective managers recognize that changes in the forces that surround a person can have great impact on that person's behavior. Unlike many of the other influence methods, this one doesn't require a large expenditure of limited resources or effort on the part of the manager on an ongoing basis. Once such a change has been successfully made, it works independently of the manager.

This method of influence is used by all managers to some degree. Many, however, use it sparingly simply because they do not have the power to change the forces acting on the person they wish to influence. In many organizations, only the top managers have the power to change the formal measurement systems, the extrinsic incentives available, the architecture, and so on.

## GENERATING AND USING POWER SUCCESSFULLY

Managers who are successful at acquiring considerable power and using it to manage their dependence on others tend to share a number of common characteristics:

1. They are sensitive to what others consider to be legitimate behavior in acquiring and using power. They recognize that the four types of power carry with them certain "obligations" regarding their acquisition and use. A person who gains a considerable amount of power based on his perceived expertise is generally expected to be an expert in certain areas. If it ever becomes publicly known that

the person is clearly not an expert in those areas, such a person will probably be labeled a "fraud" and will not only lose his power but will suffer other reprimands too.

A person with whom a number of people identify is expected to act like an ideal leader. If he clearly lets people down, he will not only lose that power, he will also suffer the righteous anger of his ex-followers. Many managers who have created or used power based on perceived dependence in ways that their employees have felt unfair, such as in requesting overtime work, have ended up with unions.

2. They have good intuitive understanding of the various types of power and methods of influence. They are sensitive to what types of power are easiest to develop with different types of people. They recognize, for example, that professionals tend to be more influenced by perceived expertise than by other forms of power. They also have a grasp of all the various methods of influence and what each can accomplish, at what costs, and with what risks. (See Exhibit 5-1.) They are good at recognizing the specific conditions in any situation and then at selecting an influence method that is compatible with those conditions.

3. They tend to develop all the types of power, to some degree, and they use all the influence methods mentioned in Exhibit 5-1. Unlike managers who are not very good at influencing people, effective managers usually do not think that only some of the methods are useful or that only some of the methods are moral. They recognize that any of the methods, used under the right circumstances, can help contribute to organizational effective-

ness with few dysfunctional consequences. At the same time, they generally try to avoid those methods that are more risky than others and those that may have dysfunctional consequences. For example, they manipulate the environment of others only when absolutely necessary.

4. They establish career goals and seek out managerial positions that allow them to successfully develop and use power. They look for jobs, for example, that use their backgrounds and skills to control or manage some critically important problem or environmental contingency that an organization faces. They recognize that success in that type of job makes others dependent on them and increases their own perceived expertise. They also seek jobs that do not demand a type or a volume of power that is inconsistent with their own skills.

5. They use all of their resources, formal authority, and power to develop still more power. To borrow Edward Banfield's metaphor, they actually look for ways to "invest" their power where they might secure a high positive return.[6] For example, by asking a person to do him two important favors, a manager might be able to finish his construction program one day ahead of schedule. That request may cost him most of the obligation-based power he has over that person, but in return he may significantly increase his perceived expertise as a manager of construction projects in the eyes of everyone in his organization.

Just as in investing money, there is always some risk involved in using power this way; it is possible to get a zero return for a sizable investment, even for the most powerful manager. Effective managers do not try to avoid risks. Instead, they look for prudent risks, just as they do when investing capital.

6. Effective managers engage in power-oriented behavior in ways that are tempered by maturity and self-control.[7] They seldom, if ever, develop and use power in impulsive ways or for their own aggrandizement.

7. Finally, they also recognize and accept as legitimate that, in using these methods, they clearly influence other people's behavior and lives. Unlike many less effective managers, they are reasonably comfortable in using power to influence people. They recognize, often only intuitively, what this article is all about—that their attempts to establish power and use it are an absolutely necessary part of the successful fulfillment of their difficult managerial role.

---

You can't learn to acquire power by rules: it has to come from inside. But by following certain rules, you can develop an awareness of it. We all have a power potential, but few of us use it, or even know it's there.

In more "primitive" cultures, youths are initiated into the rites of power, sometimes in very complicated ways. The rules are absolute and clear-cut, and must be followed exactly, but they are intended to increase the initiate's awareness of himself—simply carrying out the rituals isn't enough. If in certain American Indian tribes young men bury themselves in pits up to the neck on lonely hills in the desert, it is to learn patience, concentration, and the ability to stay motionless when

CONTINUED

necessary, however uncomfortable it may be. There's nothing mysterious about the process—a hunter who is fidgety or has to scratch himself when bitten by flies is unlikely to trap much in the way of game. Survival lies in the ability to control one's body and one's mind.

Our world is not so very different, noisy and complex as it seems, but we are less fortunate than the Indians. We are educated, at considerable expense and effort, but no wise teacher prepares us for the world we will face as adults. If we are lucky, we learn how to do a job, but for most people the price of survival is surrender. There is a place for almost everyone in our world, but usually on other people's terms rather than our own. Some of us learn how to *succeed* and may even become rich and famous; few learn how to use the world, instead of being used by it.

---

# 6

## Managing Your Boss

*John J. Gabarro and John P. Kotter*

T O MANY PEOPLE, the phrase *managing your boss* may
sound unusual or suspicious. Because of the traditional
top-down emphasis in most organizations, it is not obvious why
you need to manage relationships upward—unless, of course,
you would do so for personal or political reasons. But we are
not referring to political maneuvering or to apple polishing. We
are using the term to mean the process of consciously working
with your superior to obtain the best possible results for you,
your boss, and the company.

Recent studies suggest that effective managers take time and
effort to manage not only relationships with their subordinates
but also those with their bosses. These studies also show that

*This article was written with John J. Gabarro, the UPS Foundation Professor of Human
Resource Management at the Harvard Business School.*
*First published in the May–June 1993* Harvard Business Review.

this essential aspect of management is sometimes ignored by otherwise talented and aggressive managers. Indeed, some managers who actively and effectively supervise subordinates, products, markets, and technologies assume an almost passively reactive stance vis-à-vis their bosses. Such a stance almost always hurts them and their companies.

If you doubt the importance of managing your relationship with your boss or how difficult it is to do so effectively, consider for a moment the following sad but telling story:

Frank Gibbons was an acknowledged manufacturing genius in his industry and, by any profitability standard, a very effective executive. In 1973, his strengths propelled him into the position of vice president of manufacturing for the second largest and

*Successful managers develop relationships with everyone they depend on—including the boss.*

most profitable company in its industry. Gibbons was not, however, a good manager of people. He knew this, as did others in his company and his industry. Recognizing this weakness, the president made sure that those who reported to Gibbons were good at working with people and could compensate for his limitations. The arrangement worked well.

In 1975, Philip Bonnevie was promoted into a position reporting to Gibbons. In keeping with the previous pattern, the president selected Bonnevie because he had an excellent track record and a reputation for being good with people. In making that selection, however, the president neglected to notice that, in his rapid rise through the organization, Bonnevie had always had good-to-excellent bosses. He had never been forced to manage a relationship with a difficult boss. In retrospect, Bonnevie admits he had never thought that managing his boss was a part of his job.

Fourteen months after he started working for Gibbons, Bonnevie was fired. During that same quarter, the company reported a net loss for the first time in seven years. Many of those who were close to these events say that they don't really understand what happened. This much is known, however: while the company was bringing out a major new product—a process that required sales, engineering, and manufacturing groups to coordinate decisions very carefully—a whole series of misunderstandings and bad feelings developed between Gibbons and Bonnevie.

For example, Bonnevie claims Gibbons was aware of and had accepted Bonnevie's decision to use a new type of machinery to make the new product; Gibbons swears he did not. Furthermore, Gibbons claims he made it clear to Bonnevie that introduction of the product was too important to the company in the short run to take any major risks.

As a result of such misunderstandings, planning went awry: a new manufacturing plant was built that could not produce the new product designed by engineering, in the volume desired by sales, at a cost agreed on by the executive committee. Gibbons blamed Bonnevie for the mistake. Bonnevie blamed Gibbons.

Of course, one could argue that the problem here was caused by Gibbons's inability to manage his subordinates. But one can make just as strong a case that the problem was related to Bonnevie's inability to manage his boss. Remember, Gibbons was not having difficulty with any other subordinates. Moreover, given the personal price paid by Bonnevie (being fired and having his reputation within the industry severely tarnished), there was little consolation in saying the problem was that Gibbons was poor at managing subordinates. Everyone already knew that.

We believe that the situation could have turned out differently had Bonnevie been more adept at understanding Gibbons and at managing his relationship with him. In this case, an inability to manage upward was unusually costly. The company lost $2 million to $5 million, and Bonnevie's career was, at least temporarily, disrupted. Many less costly cases similar to this probably occur regularly in all major corporations, and the cumulative effect can be very destructive.

## MISREADING THE BOSS-SUBORDINATE RELATIONSHIP

People often dismiss stories like the one we just related as being merely cases of personality conflict. Because two people can on occasion be psychologically or temperamentally incapable of working together, this can be an apt description. But more often, we have found, a personality conflict is only a part of the problem—sometimes a very small part.

Bonnevie did not just have a different personality from Gibbons, he also made or had unrealistic assumptions and expectations about the very nature of boss-subordinate relationships. Specifically, he did not recognize that his relationship to Gibbons involved *mutual dependence* between two *fallible* human beings. Failing to recognize this, a manager typically either avoids trying to manage his or her relationship with a boss or manages it ineffectively.

Some people behave as if their bosses were not very dependent on them. They fail to see how much the boss needs their help and cooperation to do his or her job effectively. These people refuse to acknowledge that the boss can be severely hurt by their actions and needs cooperation, dependability, and honesty from them.

Some people see themselves as not very dependent on their bosses. They gloss over how much help and information they need from the boss in order to perform their own jobs well. This superficial view is particularly damaging when a manager's job and decisions affect other parts of the organization, as was the case in Bonnevie's situation. A manager's immediate boss can play a critical role in linking the manager to the rest of the organization, making sure the manager's priorities are consistent with organizational needs, and in securing the resources the manager needs to perform well. Yet

*Bosses can link managers to the rest of the organization, help them set priorities, and secure the resources they need.*

some managers need to see themselves as practically self-sufficient, as not needing the critical information and resources a boss can supply.

Many managers, like Bonnevie, assume that the boss will magically know what information or help their subordinates need and provide it to them. Certainly, some bosses do an excellent job of caring for their subordinates in this way, but for a manager to expect that from all bosses is dangerously unrealistic. A more reasonable expectation for managers to have is that modest help will be forthcoming. After all, bosses are only human. Most really effective managers accept this fact and assume primary responsibility for their own careers and development. They make a point of seeking the information and help they need to do a job instead of waiting for their bosses to provide it.

In light of the foregoing, it seems to us that managing a situation of mutual dependence among fallible human beings requires the following:

1. That you have a good understanding of the other person and yourself, especially regarding strengths, weaknesses, work styles, and needs.

2. That you use this information to develop and manage a healthy working relationship—one that is compatible with both people's work styles and assets, is characterized by mutual expectations, and meets the most critical needs of the other person. This combination is essentially what we have found highly effective managers doing.

## UNDERSTANDING THE BOSS

Managing your boss requires that you gain an understanding of the boss and his or her context, as well as your own situation. All managers do this to some degree, but many are not thorough enough.

At a minimum, you need to appreciate your boss's goals and pressures, his or her strengths and weaknesses. What are your boss's organizational and personal objectives, and what are his or her pressures, especially those from his or her own boss and others at the same level? What are your boss's long suits and blind spots? What is the preferred style of working? Does your boss like to get information through memos, formal meetings, or phone calls? Does he or she thrive on conflict or try to minimize it?

Without this information, a manager is flying blind when dealing with the boss, and unnecessary conflicts, misunderstandings, and problems are inevitable.

In one situation we studied, a top-notch marketing manager with a superior performance record was hired into a company as a vice president "to straighten out the marketing and sales problems." The company, which was having financial difficulties, had recently been acquired by a larger corporation. The president was eager to turn it around and gave the new marketing vice president free rein—at least initially. Based on his previous experience, the new vice president correctly diagnosed that greater market share was needed for the company and that strong product management was required to bring that about. Following that logic, he made a number of pricing decisions that were aimed at increasing high-volume business.

When margins declined and the financial situation did not improve, however, the president increased pressure on the new vice president. Believing that the situation would eventually correct itself as the company gained back market share, the vice president resisted the pressure.

When by the second quarter, margins and profits had still failed to improve, the president took direct control over all pricing decisions and put all items on a set level of margin, regardless of volume. The new vice president began to find himself shut out by the president, and their relationship deteriorated. In fact, the vice president found the president's behavior bizarre. Unfortunately, the president's new pricing scheme also failed to increase margins, and by the fourth quarter, both the president and the vice president were fired.

What the new vice president had not known until it was too late was that improving marketing and sales had been only *one* of the president's goals. His most immediate goal had been to make the company more profitable—quickly.

Nor had the new vice president known that his boss was invested in this short-term priority for personal as well as business reasons. The president had been a strong advocate of the acquisition within the parent company, and his personal credibility was at stake.

The vice president made three basic errors. He took information supplied to him at face value, he made assumptions in areas where he had no information, and—what was most damaging—he never actively tried to clarify what his boss's objectives were. As a result, he ended up taking actions that were actually at odds with the president's priorities and objectives.

Managers who work effectively with their bosses do not behave this way. They seek out information about the boss's goals and problems and pressures. They are alert for opportunities to question the boss and others around him or her to test their assumptions. They pay attention to clues in the boss's behavior. Although it is imperative that they do this especially when they begin working with a new boss, effective managers also do this on an ongoing basis because they recognize that priorities and concerns change.

*Managers who work effectively with their bosses are sensitive to the boss's work style.*

Being sensitive to a boss's work style can be crucial, especially when the boss is new. For example, a new president who was organized and formal in his approach replaced a man who was informal and intuitive. The new president worked best when he had written reports. He also preferred formal meetings with set agendas.

One of his division managers realized this need and worked with the new president to identify the kinds and frequency of information and reports that the president wanted. This manager also made a point of sending background information and brief agendas ahead of time for their discussions. He found that with this type of preparation their meetings were very

useful. Another interesting result was, he found that with adequate preparation his new boss was even more effective at
brainstorming problems than his more informal and intuitive
predecessor had been.

In contrast, another division manager never fully understood
how the new boss's work style differed from that of his predecessor. To the degree that he did sense it, he experienced it as
too much control. As a result, he seldom sent the new president
the background information he needed, and the president never
felt fully prepared for meetings with the manager. In fact, the
president spent much of this time when they met trying to get
information that he felt he should have had earlier. The boss
experienced these meetings as frustrating and inefficient, and
the subordinate often found himself thrown off guard by the
questions that the president asked. Ultimately, this division manager resigned.

The difference between the two division managers just described was not so much one of ability or even adaptability.
Rather, one of the men was more sensitive to his boss's work
style than the other and to the implications of his boss's needs.


## UNDERSTANDING YOURSELF

The boss is only one-half of the relationship. You are the other
half, as well as the part over which you have more direct
control. Developing an effective working relationship requires,
then, that you know your own needs, strengths and weaknesses,
and personal style.

You are not going to change either your basic personality
structure or that of your boss. But you can become aware of what
it is about you that impedes or facilitates working with your

boss and, with that awareness, take actions that make the relationship more effective.

For example, in one case we observed, a manager and his superior ran into problems whenever they disagreed. The boss's typical response was to harden his position and overstate it. The manager's reaction was then to raise the ante and intensify the forcefulness of his argument. In doing this, he channeled his anger into sharpening his attacks on the logical fallacies he saw in his boss's assumptions. His boss in turn would become even more adamant about holding his original position. Predictably, this escalating cycle resulted in the subordinate avoiding whenever possible any topic of potential conflict with his boss.

In discussing this problem with his peers, the manager discovered that his reaction to the boss was typical of how he generally reacted to counterarguments—but with a difference. His response would overwhelm his peers but not his boss. Because his attempts to discuss this problem with his boss were unsuccessful, he concluded that the only way to change the situation was to deal with his own instinctive reactions. Whenever the two reached an impasse, he would check his own impatience and suggest that they break up and think about it before getting together again. Usually when they renewed their discussion, they had digested their differences and were more able to work them through.

Gaining this level of self-awareness and acting on it are difficult but not impossible. For example, by reflecting over his past experiences, a young manager learned that he was not very good at dealing with difficult and emotional issues where people were involved. Because he disliked those issues and realized that his instinctive responses to them were seldom very good, he developed a habit of touching base with his boss whenever such a problem arose. Their discussions always surfaced ideas and approaches the manager had not considered. In many cases, they also identified specific actions the boss could take to help.

Although a superior-subordinate relationship is one of mutual dependence, it is also one in which the subordinate is typically more dependent on the boss than the other way around. This dependence inevitably results in the subordinate feeling a certain degree of frustration, sometimes anger, when his actions or options are constrained by his boss's decisions. This is a normal part of life and occurs in the best of relationships. The way in which a manager handles these frustrations largely depends on his or her predisposition toward dependence on authority figures.

*The counterdependent manager sometimes sees the boss as an institutional enemy.*

Some people's instinctive reaction under these circumstances is to resent the boss's authority and to rebel against the boss's decisions. Sometimes a person will escalate a conflict beyond what is appropriate. Seeing the boss almost as an institutional enemy, this type of manager will often, without being conscious of it, fight with the boss just for the sake of fighting. The subordinate's reactions to being constrained are usually strong and sometimes impulsive. He or she sees the boss as someone who, by virtue of the role, is a hindrance to progress, an obstacle to be circumvented or at best tolerated.

Psychologists call this pattern of reactions counterdependent behavior. Although a counterdependent person is difficult for most superiors to manage and usually has a history of strained relationships with superiors, this sort of manager is apt to have even more trouble with a boss who tends to be directive or authoritarian. When the manager acts on his or her negative feelings, often in subtle and nonverbal ways, the boss sometimes does become the enemy. Sensing the subordinate's latent hostility, the boss will lose trust in the subordinate or his or her judgment and then behave even less openly.

Paradoxically, a manager with this type of predisposition is often a good manager of his or her own people. He or she will many times go out of the way to get support for them and will not hesitate to go to bat for them.

At the other extreme are managers who swallow their anger and behave in a very compliant fashion when the boss makes what they know to be a poor decision. These managers will agree with the boss even when a disagreement might be welcome or when the boss would easily alter a decision if given more information. Because they bear no relationship to the specific situation at hand, their responses are as much an overreaction as those of counterdependent managers. Instead of seeing the boss as an enemy, these people deny their anger—the other extreme—and tend to see the boss as if he or she were an all-wise parent who should know best, should take responsibility for their careers, train them in all they need to know, and protect them from overly ambitious peers.

Both counterdependence and overdependence lead managers to hold unrealistic views of what a boss is. Both views ignore that most bosses, like everyone else, are imperfect and fallible. They don't have unlimited time, encyclopedic knowledge, or extrasensory perception; nor are they evil enemies. They have their own pressures and concerns that are sometimes at odds with the wishes of the subordinate—and often for good reason.

Altering predispositions toward authority, especially at the extremes, is almost impossible without intensive psychotherapy (psychoanalytic theory and research suggest that such predispositions are deeply rooted in a person's personality and upbringing). However, an awareness of these extremes and the range between them can be very useful in understanding where your own predispositions fall and what the implications are for how you tend to behave in relation to your boss.

If you believe, on the one hand, that you have some tendencies toward counterdependence, you can understand and even predict what your reactions and overreactions are likely to be. If, on the other hand, you believe you have some tendencies toward overdependence, you might question the extent to which your overcompliance or inability to confront real differences may be making both you and your boss less effective.

## DEVELOPING AND MANAGING
## THE RELATIONSHIP

With a clear understanding of both your boss and yourself, you can *usually* establish a way of working together that fits both of you, that is characterized by unambiguous mutual expectations, and that helps you both be more productive and effective. Exhibit 6-1 summarizes some things such a relationship consists of. Following are a few more.

### Compatible Work Styles

Above all else, a good working relationship with a boss accommodates differences in work style. For example, in one situation we studied, a manager (who had a relatively good relationship with his superior) realized that during meetings his boss would often become inattentive and sometimes brusque. The subordinate's own style tended to be discursive and exploratory. He would often digress from the topic at hand to deal with background factors, alternative approaches, and so forth.

EXHIBIT 6-1

## Checklist for Managing Your Boss

**Make sure you understand your boss and his or her context, including:**

☐ Goals and objectives
☐ Pressures
☐ Strengths, weaknesses, blind spots
☐ Preferred work style

**Assess yourself and your needs, including:**

☐ Strengths and weaknesses
☐ Personal style
☐ Predisposition toward dependence on authority figures

**Develop and maintain a relationship that:**

☐ Fits both your needs and styles
☐ Is characterized by mutual expectations
☐ Keeps your boss informed
☐ Is based on dependability and honesty
☐ Selectively uses your boss's time and resources

His boss preferred to discuss problems with a minimum of background detail and became impatient and distracted whenever his subordinate digressed from the immediate issue.

Recognizing this difference in style, the manager became terser and more direct during meetings with his boss. To help himself do this, before meetings, he would develop brief agendas that he used as a guide. Whenever he felt that a digression was needed, he explained why. This small shift in his own style made these meetings more effective and far less frustrating for both of them.

Subordinates can adjust their styles in response to their bosses' preferred method for receiving information. Peter Drucker divides bosses into "listeners" and "readers." Some bosses like to get information in report form so they can read and study it.

Others work better with information and reports presented in person so they can ask questions. As Drucker points out, the implications are obvious. If your boss is a listener, you brief him or her in person, *then* follow it up with a memo. If your boss is a reader, you cover important items or proposals in a memo or report, *then* discuss them.

Other adjustments can be made according to a boss's decision-making style. Some bosses prefer to be involved in decisions and problems as they arise. These are high-involvement managers who like to keep their hands on the pulse of the operation. Usually their needs (and your own) are best satisfied if you touch base with them on an ad hoc basis. A boss who has a need to be involved will become involved one way or another, so there are advantages to including him or her at your initiative. Other bosses prefer to delegate—they don't want to be involved. They expect you to come to them with major problems and inform them about any important changes.

Creating a compatible relationship also involved drawing on each other's strengths and making up for each other's weaknesses. Because he knew that the boss—the vice president of engineering—was not very good at monitoring his employees' problems, one manager we studied made a point of doing it himself. The stakes were high: the engineers and technicians were all union members, the company worked on a customer-contract basis, and the company had recently experienced a serious strike.

The manager worked closely with his boss, along with people in the scheduling department and the personnel office, to make sure that potential problems were avoided. He also developed an informal arrangement through which his boss would review with him any proposed changes in personnel or assignment policies before taking action. The boss valued his advice

and credited his subordinate for improving both the performance of the division and the labor-management climate.

## Mutual Expectations

The subordinate who passively assumes that he or she knows
what the boss expects is in for trouble. Of course, some superiors
will spell out their expectations very explicitly and in great
detail. But most do not. And although many corporations
have systems that provide a basis for communicating expectations (such as formal planning processes, career planning reviews,
and performance appraisal reviews), these systems never work
perfectly. Also, between these formal reviews, expectations
invariably change.

Ultimately, the burden falls on the subordinate to find out
what the boss's expectations are. They can be both broad (such
as what kinds of problems the boss wishes to be informed about
and when) as well as very specific (such things as when a
particular project should be completed and what kinds of information the boss needs in the interim).

Getting a boss who tends to be vague or not explicit to express
expectations can be difficult. But effective managers find ways to
get that information. Some will draft a detailed memo covering
key aspects of their work and then send it to their boss for
approval. They then follow this up with a face-to-face discussion
in which they go over each item in the memo. A discussion like
this will often surface virtually all of the boss's expectations.

Other effective managers will deal with an inexplicit boss by
initiating an ongoing series of informal discussions about
"good management" and "our objectives." Still others find useful
information more indirectly through those who used to work

for the boss and through the formal planning systems in which the boss makes commitments to his or her own superior. Which approach you choose, of course, should depend on your understanding of your boss's style.

Developing a workable set of mutual expectations also requires that you communicate your own expectations to the boss, find out if they are realistic, and influence the boss to accept the ones that are important to you. Being able to influence the boss to value your expectations can be particularly important if the boss is an overachiever. Such a boss will often set unrealistically high standards that need to be brought into line with reality.

## A Flow of Information

How much information a boss needs about what a subordinate is doing will vary significantly depending on the boss's style, the situation he or she is in, and the confidence the boss has in the subordinate. But it is not uncommon for a boss to need more information than the subordinate would naturally supply or for the subordinate to think the boss knows more than he or she really does. Effective managers recognize that they probably underestimate what their bosses need to know and make sure they find ways to keep them informed through processes that fit their styles.

Managing the flow of information upward is particularly difficult if the boss does not like to hear about problems. Although many people would deny it, bosses often give off signals they want to hear only good news. They show great displeasure— usually nonverbally—when someone tells them about a problem. Ignoring individual achievement, they may even evaluate more favorably subordinates who do not bring problems to them.

Nevertheless, for the good of the organization, the boss, and the subordinate, a superior needs to hear about failures as well as successes. Some subordinates deal with a good-news-only boss by finding indirect ways to get the necessary information to him or her, such as a management information system. Others see to it that potential problems, whether in the form of good surprises or bad news, are communicated immediately.

## Dependability and Honesty

Few things are more disabling to a boss than a subordinate on whom he cannot depend, whose work he cannot trust. Almost no one is intentionally undependable, but many managers are inadvertently so because of oversight or uncertainty about the boss's priorities. A commitment to an optimistic delivery date may please a superior in the short term but become a source of displeasure if not honored. It's difficult for a boss to rely on a subordinate who repeatedly slips deadlines. As one president (describing a subordinate) put it: "I'd rather he be more consistent even if he delivered fewer peak successes—at least I could rely on him."

Nor are many managers intentionally dishonest with their bosses. But it is easy to shade the truth and play down issues. Current concerns often become future surprise problems. It's almost impossible for bosses to work effectively if they cannot rely on a fairly accurate reading from their subordinates. Because it undermines credibility, dishonesty is perhaps the most troubling trait a subordinate can have. Without a basic level of trust, a boss feels compelled to check all of a subordinate's decisions, which makes it difficult to delegate.

## Good Use of Time and Resources

Your boss is probably as limited in his or her store of time, energy, and influence as you are. Every request you make of your boss uses up some of these resources, so it's wise to draw on these resources selectively. This may sound obvious, but many managers use up their boss's time (and some of their own credibility) over relatively trivial issues.

One vice president went to great lengths to get his boss to fire a meddlesome secretary in another department. His boss had to use considerable influence to do it. Understandably, the head of the other department was not pleased. Later, when the vice president wanted to tackle more important problems, he ran into trouble. By using up blue chips on a relatively trivial issue, he had made it difficult for him and his boss to meet more important goals.

No doubt, some subordinates will resent that on top of all their other duties, they also need to take time and energy to manage their relationships with their bosses. Such managers fail to realize the importance of this activity and how it can simplify their jobs by eliminating potentially severe problems. Effective managers recognize that this part of their work is legitimate. Seeing themselves as ultimately responsible for what they achieve in an organization, they know they need to establish and manage relationships with everyone on whom they depend—and that includes the boss.

# 7

# What Effective General Managers Really Do

H ERE IS A DESCRIPTION of a reasonably typical day in the life of a successful executive. The individual in this case is Michael Richardson, the president of an investment management firm.

**A.M. 7:35**  He arrives at work after a short commute, unpacks his briefcase, gets some coffee, and begins a "to do" list for the day.

**7:40**  Jerry Bradshaw, a subordinate, arrives at his office, which is right next to Richardson's. One of Bradshaw's duties is to act as an assistant to Richardson.

**7:45**  Bradshaw and Richardson converse about a number of topics. Richardson shows Bradshaw some pictures he recently took at his summer home.

**8:00**  Bradshaw and Richardson talk about a schedule and priorities for the day. In the process, they touch on a dozen

---

*First published in the November–December 1982 Harvard Business Review.*

different subjects and issues relating to customers, and other subordinates.

**8:20** Frank Wilson, another subordinate, drops in. He asks a few questions about a personnel problem and then joins in the ongoing discussion. The discussion is straightforward, rapid, and occasionally punctuated with humor.

**8:30** Fred Holly, the chairman of the firm and Richardson's "boss," stops in and joins in the conversation. He asks about an appointment scheduled for 11 o'clock and brings up a few other topics as well.

**8:40** Richardson leaves to get more coffee. Bradshaw, Holly, and Wilson continue their conversation.

**8:42** Richardson comes back. A subordinate of a subordinate stops in and says hello. The others leave.

**8:43** Bradshaw drops off a report, hands Richardson instructions that go with it, and leaves.

**8:45** Joan Swanson, Richardson's secretary, arrives. They discuss her new apartment and arrangements for a meeting later in the morning.

**8:49** Richardson gets a phone call from a subordinate who is returning a call from the day before. They talk primarily about the subject of the report Richardson just received.

**8:55** He leaves his office and goes to a regular morning meeting that one of his subordinates runs. There are about 30 people there. Richardson reads during the meeting.

**9:09** The meeting is over. Richardson stops one of the people there and talks to him briefly.

**9:15** He walks over to the office of one of his subordinates, who is corporate counsel. His boss, Holly, is there too. They discuss a phone call the lawyer just received. While standing, the three talk about possible responses to a problem. As before, the exchange is quick and includes some humor.

**9:30** Richardson goes back to his office for a meeting with the vice chairman of another firm (a potential customer and supplier). One other person, a liaison with that firm and a subordinate's subordinate, also attends the meeting. The discussion is cordial. It covers many topics, from their products to U.S. foreign relations.

**9:50** The visitor and the subordinate's subordinate leave. Richardson opens the adjoining door to Bradshaw's office and asks a question.

**9:52** Richardson's secretary comes in with five items of business.

**9:55** Bradshaw drops in, asks a question about a customer, and then leaves.

**9:58** Frank Wilson and one of his people arrive. He gives Richardson a memo and then the three talk about the important legal problem. Wilson does not like a decision that Richardson has tentatively made and urges him to reconsider. The discussion goes back and forth for 20 minutes until they agree on the next action and schedule it for 9 o'clock the next day.

**10:35** They leave. Richardson looks over papers on his desk, then picks one up and calls Holly's secretary regarding the minutes of the last board meeting. He asks her to make a few corrections.

**10:41** His secretary comes in with a card for a friend who is sick. He writes a note to go with the card.

**10:50** He gets a brief phone call, then goes back to the papers on his desk.

**11:03** His boss stops in. Before Richardson and Holly can begin to talk, Richardson gets another call. After the call, he tells his secretary that someone didn't get a letter he sent and asks her to send another.

**11:05** Holly brings up a couple of issues, and then Bradshaw comes in. The three start talking about Jerry Phillips, who has become a difficult problem. Bradshaw leads the conversation, telling the others what he has done during the last few days regarding this issue. Richardson and Holly ask questions. After a while, Richardson begins to take notes. The exchange, as before, is rapid and straightforward. They try to define the problem and outline possible alternative next steps. Richardson lets the discussion roam away from and back to the topic again and again. Finally, they agree on a next step.

**P.M. 12:00**   Richardson orders lunch for himself and Bradshaw. Bradshaw comes in and goes over a dozen items. Wilson stops by to say that he has already followed up on their earlier conversation.

**12:10**   A staff person stops by with some calculations Richardson had requested. He thanks her and has a brief, amicable conversation.

**12:20**   Lunch arrives. Richardson and Bradshaw go into the conference room to eat. Over lunch they pursue business and nonbusiness subjects. They laugh often at each other's humor. They end the lunch talking about a potential major customer.

**1:15**   Back in Richardson's office, they continue the discussion about the customer. Bradshaw gets a pad, and they go over in detail a presentation to the customer. Then Bradshaw leaves.

**1:40**   Working at his desk, Richardson looks over a new marketing brochure.

**1:50**   Bradshaw comes in again; he and Richardson go over another dozen details regarding the presentation to the potential customer. Bradshaw leaves.

**1:55**   Jerry Thomas comes in. He is a subordinate of Richardson, and he has scheduled for the afternoon some key performance appraisals, which he and Richardson will hold in Richardson's office. They talk briefly about how they will handle each appraisal.

**2:00** Fred Jacobs (a subordinate of Thomas) joins Richardson and Thomas. Thomas runs the meeting. He goes over Jacobs's bonus for the year and the reason for it. Then the three of them talk about Jacobs's role in the upcoming year. They generally agree and Jacobs leaves.

**2:30** Jane Kimble comes in. The appraisal follows the same format as for Fred Jacobs. Richardson asks a lot of questions and praises Kimble at times. The meeting ends on a friendly note of agreement.

**3:00** George Houston comes in; the appraisal format is repeated again.

**3:30** When Houston leaves, Richardson and Thomas talk briefly about how well they have accomplished their objectives in the meetings. Then they talk briefly about some of Thomas's other subordinates. Thomas leaves.

**3:45** Richardson gets a short phone call. His secretary and Bradshaw come in with a list of requests.

**3:50** Richardson receives a call from Jerry Phillips. He gets his notes from the 11 o'clock meeting about Phillips. They go back and forth on the phone talking about lost business, unhappy subordinates, who did what to whom, and what should be done now. It is a long, circular, and sometimes emotional conversation. Near the end, Phillips is agreeing with Richardson on the next step and thanking him.

**4:55** Bradshaw, Wilson, and Holly all step in. Each is following up on different issues that were discussed earlier in the day. Richardson briefly tells them of his conversation with Phillips. Bradshaw and Holly leave.

**5:10** Richardson and Wilson have a light conversation about three or four items.

**5:20**   Jerry Thomas stops in. He describes a new personnel problem and the three of them discuss it. More and more humor starts coming into the conversation. They agree on an action to take.

**5:30**   Richardson begins to pack his briefcase. Five people briefly stop by, one or two at a time.

**5:45**   He leaves the office.

In at least a dozen ways, Richardson's day is typical for a general manager. The daily behavior of the successful GMs I have studied generally conforms to these patterns (for a description, see "Basis of the Study" at the end of this chapter):

**1.**   They spend most of their time with others. The average GM spends only 25% of his working time alone, and this is spent largely at home, on airplanes, or while commuting. Few spend less than 70% of their time with others, and some spend up to 90% of their work time this way.

**2.**   The people they spend time with include many in addition to their direct subordinates and boss. GMs regularly go around the formal chain of command. They also regularly see people who often appear to be unimportant outsiders.

**3.**   The breadth of topics in these discussions is extremely wide. The GMs do not limit their focus to planning, business strategy, staffing, and other "top management concerns." They discuss virtually anything and everything even remotely associated with their businesses and organizations.

**4.**   In these conversations, GMs typically ask a lot of questions. In a half-hour conversation, some will ask literally hundreds.

5. During these conversations, the GMs rarely seem to make "big" decisions.

6. These discussions usually contain a considerable amount of joking and kidding and concern nonwork-related issues. The humor is often about others in the organization or industry. Nonwork discussions are usually about people's families, hobbies, or recent outside activities (e.g., golf scores).

7. In not a small number of these encounters, the substantive issue discussed is relatively unimportant to the business or organization. That is, GMs regularly engage in activities that even they regard as a waste of time.

8. In these encounters, the executives rarely give orders in a traditional sense. That is, they seldom "tell" people what to do.

9. Nevertheless, GMs frequently engage in attempts to influence others. However, instead of telling people what to do, they ask, request, cajole, persuade, and intimidate.

10. In allocating their time with others, GMs often react to others' initiatives. Much of the typical GM's day is unplanned. Even GMs who have a heavy schedule of planned meetings often end up spending a lot of time on topics that are not on the official agenda.

11. Most of their time with others is spent in short, disjointed conversations. Discussions of a single question or issue rarely last more than ten minutes. And it is not at all unusual for a GM to cover ten unrelated topics in a five-minute interaction.

12. They work long hours. The average person I have studied works just under 60 hours per week. Not many work fewer than 55 hours per week. Although some of their work is done

at home, while commuting to work, or while traveling, they spend most of their time at their places of work.

These patterns in daily behavior, which Richardson's day illustrate, are basically consistent with other studies of managerial behavior,[1] especially those of high-level managers.[2] Nevertheless, as Henry Mintzberg has pointed out,[3] this behavior seems hard to reconcile, on the surface at least, with traditional notions of what top managers do (or should do). It is hard to fit the behavior into categories like "planning," "organizing," "controlling," "directing," "staffing," and so on.

And even if one tries, two conclusions surface: (1) The "planning" and "organizing" that these people do does not seem very systematically done; it seems rather hit or miss, rather sloppy. (2) A lot of behavior ends up being classified as "none of the above." The implication is that these are things that top managers should not be doing. Nevertheless, hit or miss is precisely how planning and organizing manifest themselves in the daily behavior of effective executives, and for perfectly understandable reasons.

## HOW EFFECTIVE EXECUTIVES
## APPROACH THEIR JOBS

To understand why effective GMs behave as they do, it is essential first to recognize the types of challenges and dilemmas found in most of their jobs, the two most fundamental of which are:

- Figuring out what to do despite uncertainty, great diversity, and an enormous amount of potentially relevant information.

- Getting things done through a large and diverse set of people despite having little direct control over most of them.

The severity of these challenges in complex organizations is much greater than most nonexecutives would suspect. And the implications of these job demands for the traditional management functions of planning, staffing, organizing, directing, and controlling are very powerful.

Exhibit 7-1 suggests that the very nature of executive jobs requires a complex and subtle approach to planning, organizing, staffing, and so forth. The approach needs to take into account the uncertainty involved, as well as the diversity and volume of potentially relevant information. It must also come to grips with the difficult human environment; it must somehow help executives get things done despite their dependency on a large number of people, many of whom are not their subordinates.

An examination of effective general managers suggests that they have found just such an approach, a central part of which might be usefully thought of as "agenda setting" and "network building."

## AGENDA SETTING

During their first six months to a year in a new job, GMs usually spend considerable time establishing their agendas. Later, they continue to update them but in a less time-consuming process.

Effective executives develop agendas that are made up of loosely connected goals and plans that address their long-, medium-, and short-term responsibilities. The agendas usually

EXHIBIT 7-1

## Behavioral Implications, Given the Nature of GM Jobs, for the Traditional Management Functions

| Implications for Traditional Management Functions | Dilemmas Inherent in the Job | |
|---|---|---|
| | **Figuring out what to do** despite great uncertainty, great diversity, and an enormous quantity of potentially relevant information. | **Getting things done** through a large and diverse group of people despite having little direct control over most of them. |
| **Planning** | Planning is very difficult to do well in such a context. It requires a lot of time and attention, not just a series of meetings once a year. It requires some good information systems to sort out the noise and focus on essential data. | Planning must be done in a way that does not exacerbate the already very difficult human environment. One must therefore be very careful regarding what is put on paper or said to others. |
| **Staffing and Organizing** | Some type of sound plan or map is essential, because without it there is no rational basis for "staffing" and "organizing." | The resources one needs to get the job done include many people besides direct subordinates. Hence, some form of "staffing" and "organizing" activity must be aimed at many others and this activity will have to rely mainly on methods other than formal staffing and organizing procedures. |
| **Directing and Controlling** | Some type of sound plan or map is essential, because without it, it is impossible to know where to direct one's attention among the infinite possibilities. Without it, one cannot know what to direct or control. | A fairly strong set of cooperative relationships to those resources on which one is dependent is essential, or one simply will not be able to "direct" and "control." |

address a broad range of financial, product / market, and organizational issues. They include both vague and specific items. Exhibit 7-2 summarizes the contents of a typical GM's agenda.

Although most corporations today have formal planning processes that produce written plans, GMs' agendas always

EXHIBIT 7-2

## A GM's Typical Agenda

| Time Frame | Key Issues | | |
|---|---|---|---|
| | Financial | Business Product / Market | Organizational People |
| Long run 5 to 20 years | A vague notion of revenues or ROI desired in 10 to 20 years. | Only a vague notion of what kind of business (products and markets) the GM wants to develop. | Vague; sometimes includes a notion about the type of company GM wants and the caliber of management that will be needed. |
| Medium run 1 to 5 years | A fairly specific set of goals for sales and income and ROI for the next five years. | Some goals and plans for growing the business, such as: (a) introduce three new products before 1985, and (b) explore acquisition possibilities in the communication industry. | A short list of items, such as: (a) by 1983 we will need a major reorganization, and (b) find a replacement for Corey by 1984. |
| Short run 0 to 12 months | A very detailed list of financial objectives for the quarter and the year in all financial areas: sales, expenses, income, ROI, and so on. | A set of general objectives and plans aimed at such things as: (a) the market share for various products, and (b) the inventory levels of various lines. | A list of items, such as: (a) find a replacement for Smith soon, and (b) get Jones to commit himself to a more aggressive set of five-year objectives. |

include goals, priorities, strategies, and plans that are not in these documents. This is not to say that formal plans and the GMs' agendas are incompatible. Generally they are very consistent, but they differ in at least three important ways.

- First, the formal plans tend to be written mostly in terms of detailed financial numbers. GMs' agendas tend to be less detailed in financial objectives and more detailed in strategies and plans for the business or the organization.

- Second, formal plans usually focus entirely on the short and moderate run (3 months to 5 years), while GMs' agendas tend to focus on a broader time frame, which includes the immediate future (1 to 30 days) and the longer run (5 to 20 years).

- Finally, the formal plans tend to be more explicit, rigorous, and logical, especially regarding how various financial items fit together. GMs' agendas often contain lists of goals or plans that are not as explicitly connected.

Executives begin the process of developing these agendas immediately after starting their jobs, if not before. They use their knowledge of the businesses and organizations involved along with new information received each day to quickly develop a rough agenda—typically, this contains a very loosely connected and incomplete set of objectives, along with a few specific strategies and plans. Then over time, as more and more information is gathered, they incrementally (one step at a time) make the agendas more complete and more tightly connected.

In gathering information to set their agendas, effective GMs rely more on discussions with others than on books, magazines, or reports. These people tend to be individuals with whom they have relationships, not necessarily people in the "appropriate" job or function (e.g., such as a person in the planning function). In this way, they obtain information continuously, day after day, not just at planning meetings. And they do so by using their current knowledge of the business and organization and of management in general to help them direct their questioning, not by asking broad or general questions. In other words, they find ways within the flow of their workdays to ask a few critical questions and to receive in return some information that would be useful for agenda-setting purposes.

With this information, GMs make agenda-setting decisions both consciously (or analytically) and unconsciously (or intuitively) in a process that is largely internal to their minds. Indeed, important agenda-setting decisions are often not observable. In selecting specific activities to include in their agendas, GMs look for those that accomplish multiple goals, that are consistent with all other goals and plans, and that are within their power to implement. Projects and programs that seem important and logical but do not meet these criteria tend to be discarded or are at least resisted.

Almost all effective GMs seem to use this type of agenda-setting process, but the best performers do so to a greater degree and with more skill. For example, the "excellent" performers I have studied develop agendas based on more explicit business strategies that address longer time frames and that include a wider range of business issues. They do so by more aggressively seeking information from others (including "bad news"), by more skillfully asking questions, and by more successfully seeking out programs and projects that can help accomplish multiple objectives at once.[4]

## NETWORK BUILDING

In addition to setting agendas, effective GMs allocate significant time and effort when they first take their jobs to developing a network of cooperative relationships among those people they feel are needed to satisfy their emerging agendas. Even after the first six months, this activity still takes up considerable time;

but generally, it is most intense during the first months in a job. After that, their attention shifts toward using the networks to both implement and help in updating the agendas.

This network-building activity, as I have observed it and had it described to me, is aimed at much more than just direct subordinates. GMs develop cooperative relationships with and among peers, outsiders, their bosses' boss, and their subordinates' subordinates. Indeed, they develop relationships with (and sometimes among) any and all of the hundreds or even thousands of people on whom they feel dependent because of their jobs. That is, just as they create an agenda that is different from, although generally consistent with, formal plans, they also create a network that is different from, but generally consistent with, the formal organization structure (see Exhibit 7-3 for a typical GM's network).

In these large networks, the nature of the relationships varies significantly in intensity and in type; some relationships are much stronger than others, some much more personal than others, and so on. Indeed, to some degree, every relationship in a network is different because it has a unique history, it is between unique people, and so forth.

GMs develop these networks of cooperative relationships using a wide variety of face-to-face methods. They try to make others feel legitimately obliged to them by doing favors or by stressing their formal relationships. They act in ways to encourage others to identify with them. They carefully nurture their professional reputations in the eyes of others. They even maneuver to make others feel that they are particularly dependent on the GMs for resources, or career advancement, or other support.

In addition to developing relationships with existing personnel, effective GMs also often develop their networks by moving, hiring, and firing subordinates. Generally, they do so to

**EXHIBIT 7-3**

# A Typical General Manager's Network

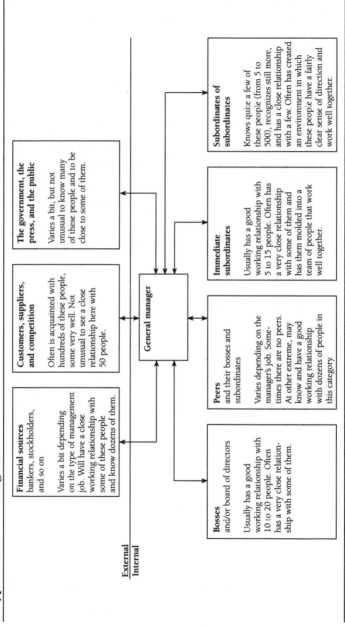

**External**
**Internal**

**Financial sources**
bankers, stockholders, and so on

Varies a bit depending on the type of management job. Will have a close working relationship with some of these people and know dozens of them.

**Customers, suppliers, and competition**

Often is acquainted with hundreds of these people, some very well. Not unusual to see a close relationship here with 50 people.

**The government, the press, and the public**

Varies a bit, but not unusual to know many of these people and to be close to some of them.

**General manager**

**Bosses**
and/or board of directors

Usually has a good working relationship with 10 to 20 people. Often has a very close relationship with some of them.

**Peers**
and their bosses and subordinates

Varies depending on the manager's job. Sometimes there are no peers. At other extreme, may know and have a good working relationship with dozens of people in this category.

**Immediate subordinates**

Usually has a good working relationship with 5 to 15 people. Often has a very close relationship with some of them and has them molded into a team of people that work well together.

**Subordinates of subordinates**

Knows quite a few of these people (from 5 to 500), recognizes still more, and has a close relationship with a few. Often has created an environment in which these people have a fairly clear sense of direction and work well together.

strengthen their ability to get things done. In a similar way, they also change suppliers or bankers, lobby to get different people into peer positions, and even restructure their boards to improve their relationship with a needed resource.

Furthermore, they also sometimes shape their networks by trying to create certain types of relationships *among* the people in various parts of the network. That is, they try to create the appropriate "environment" (norms and values) they feel is necessary to implement their agendas. Typically this is an environment in which people are willing to work hard on the GM's agenda and cooperate for the greater good. Although executives sometimes try to create such an environment among peers, bosses, or outsiders, they do so most often among their subordinates.

Almost all effective GMs use this network-building process, but the best performers do so more aggressively and more skillfully. "Excellent" performers, for example, create networks with many talented people in them and with strong ties to and among their subordinates. They do so by using a wide variety of methods with great skill. The "good / fair" performers tend to use fewer network-building methods, employ them less aggressively, and in the process, create weaker networks.[5]

## EXECUTION: GETTING NETWORKS TO IMPLEMENT AGENDAS

After they have largely developed their networks and agendas, effective GMs tend to shift their attention toward using the networks to implement their agendas. In doing so, they marshal their interpersonal skills, budgetary resources, and information to influence people and events in a variety of direct and indirect ways.

In implementing their agendas, GMs often call on virtually their entire network of relationships to help them. They do not limit their assistance to direct subordinates and a boss; when necessary, they use any and all of their relationships. During my time with GMs, I have seen some of them call on peers, corporate staff people, subordinates reporting three or four levels below them, bosses reporting two or three levels above them, suppliers or customers, even competitors, to help them get something done. There is no category of people that was never used. And in each case, the basic pattern was the same:

The GM was trying to get some action on items in his agenda that he felt would not be accomplished without intervention on his part.

- The people he approached could be of help, often uniquely so.
- The people he approached were part of his network.
- The GM chose people and an approach with an eye toward achieving multiple objectives at once and doing so without inadvertently disturbing important relationships in the network.

Having approached people, GMs often influence them by simply asking or suggesting that they do something, knowing that because of their relationship with the person, he or she will comply. In some cases, depending on the issue involved and the nature of the relationship, they also use their knowledge and information to help persuade these people. Under other circumstances, they will use resources available to them to negotiate a trade. And occasionally, they even resort to intimidation and coercion.

Effective GMs also often use their networks to exert indirect influence on people, including people who are not a part of that network. In some cases, GMs will convince one person who is in their network to get a second, who is not, to take some needed action. More indirectly still, GMs will sometimes approach a number of different people, requesting them to take actions that would then shape events that influence other individuals. Perhaps the most common example of indirect influence involves staging an event of some sort. In a typical case, the GM would set up a meeting or meetings and influence others through the selection of participants, the choice of an agenda, and often by his own participation.

Unlike the case of direct influence, GMs achieve much of their more indirect influence through symbolic methods. That is, they use meetings, architecture, language, stories about the organization, time, and space as symbols in order to get some message across indirectly.

All effective GMs seem to get things done this way, but the best performers do so more than others and with greater skill. That is, the better performers tend to mobilize more people to get more things done, and do so using a wider range of influence tactics. "Excellent" performers ask, encourage, cajole, praise, reward, demand, manipulate, and generally motivate others with great skill in face-to-face situations. They also rely more heavily on indirect influence than the "good" managers, who tend to rely on a more narrow range of influence techniques and apply them with less finesse.[6]

## HOW THE JOB DETERMINES
## BEHAVIOR

Most of the visible patterns in daily behavior seem to be direct consequences of the way GMs approach their job, and thus consequences of the nature of the job itself and the type of people involved. More specifically, some of these patterns seem to derive from the approach taken to agenda setting, others from network building, others from how they tend to use networks to implement agendas, and still others from the approach in general.

Spending most of the time with others (pattern 1) seems to be a natural consequence of the GM's overall approach to the job and the central role the network of relationships plays. As we saw earlier, GMs develop a network of relationships with those the job makes them dependent on and then use that network to help create, implement, and update an organizational agenda. As such, the whole approach to the job involves interacting with people. Hence it should not be surprising to find that on a daily basis, GMs spend most of their time with others.

Likewise, because the network tends to include all those the GM is dependent on, it is hardly surprising to find the GM spending time with many besides a boss and direct subordinates (pattern 2). And because the agenda tends to include items related to all the long-, medium-, and short-run responsibilities associated with the job, it is to be expected that the breadth of topics covered in daily conversations might be very wide (pattern 3).

A few of the other patterns seem to be a direct consequence of the agenda-setting approach employed by GMs. As we saw earlier, agenda setting involves gathering information on a continuous basis from network members, usually by asking questions. That GMs ask a lot of questions (pattern 4) follows directly. With the information in hand, we saw that GMs create largely unwritten agendas. Hence, major agenda-setting decisions are often invisible; they occur in the GM's mind (pattern 5).

We also saw that network building involves the use of a wide range of interpersonal tactics. Since humor and nonwork discussions can be used as effective tools for building relationships and maintaining them under stressful conditions, we should not be surprised to find these tools used often (as we do—pattern 6). Since maintaining relationships requires that one deal with issues that other people feel are important (regardless of their centrality to the business), it is also not surprising to find the GMs spending time on substantive issues that seem unimportant to us and them (pattern 7).

As I indicated earlier, after the initial period on the job the thrust of the GMs' approach is to use their networks to implement their agendas. They do so using a wide variety of direct and indirect influence methods. Ordering is only one of many methods. Under these circumstances, one would expect to find them rarely ordering others (pattern 8) but spending a lot of time trying to influence others (pattern 9).

## THE EFFICIENCY OF SEEMINGLY INEFFICIENT BEHAVIOR

Of all the patterns visible in daily behavior, perhaps the most difficult to understand, or at least appreciate, are that the executives do not plan their days in advance in much detail but instead react (pattern 10) and that conversations are short and disjointed (pattern 11). On the surface at least, behaving this way seems particularly unmanagerial. Yet these patterns are possibly the most important and efficient of all.

The following is a typical example of the effectiveness and efficiency of "reactive" behavior. On his way to a meeting, a GM bumped into a staff member who did not report to him. Using this opportunity, in a two-minute conversation he: (a) asked two questions and received the information he needed; (b) reinforced their good relationship by sincerely complimenting the staff member on something he had recently done; and (c) got the staff member to agree to do something that the GM needed done.

The agenda in his mind guided the executive through this encounter, prompting him to ask important questions and to request an important action. And his relationship with this member of his network allowed him to get the cooperation he needed to do all this very quickly. Had he tried to plan this encounter in advance, he would have had to set up and attend a meeting, which would have taken at least 15 to 30 minutes, or 750% to 1,500% more time than the chance encounter. And if he had not already had a good relationship with the person, the meeting may have taken even longer or been ineffective.

In a similar way, agendas and networks allow GMs to engage in short and disjointed conversations, which can be extremely efficient. The following set of very short discussions, taken from a day in the life of John Thompson, a division manager in a financial services corporation, is typical in this regard. The conversation occurred one morning in Thompson's office. With him were two of his subordinates, Phil Dodge and Jud Smith.

*Thompson:* "What about Potter?"
*Dodge:* "He's OK."

| | |
|---|---|
| *Smith:* | "Don't forget about Chicago." |
| *Dodge:* | "Oh yeah." [Makes a note to himself.] |
| *Thompson:* | "OK. Then what about next week?" |
| *Dodge:* | "We're set." |
| *Thompson:* | "Good. By the way, how is Ted doing?" |
| *Smith:* | "Better. He got back from the hospital on Tuesday. Phyllis says he looks good." |
| *Thompson:* | "That's good to hear. I hope he doesn't have a relapse." |
| *Dodge:* | "I'll see you this afternoon." [Leaves the room.] |
| *Thompson:* | "OK. [To Smith.] Are we all set for now?" |
| *Smith:* | "Yeah." [He gets up and starts to leave.] |
| *Lawrence:* | [Steps into the doorway from the hall and speaks to Thompson.] "Have you seen the April numbers yet?" |
| *Thompson:* | "No, have you?" |
| *Lawrence:* | "Yes, five minutes ago. They're good except for CD, which is off by 5%." |
| *Thompson:* | "That's better than I expected." |
| *Smith:* | "I bet George is happy." |
| *Thompson:* | [Laughing.] "If he is, he won't be after I talk to him." [Turner, Thompson's secretary, sticks her head through the doorway and tells him Bill Larson is on the phone.] |
| *Thompson:* | "I'll take it. Will you ask George to stop by later? [Others leave and Thompson picks up the phone.] Bill, good morning, how are you? . . . Yeah. . . . Is that right? . . . No, don't worry about it. I think about a million and a half. Yeah. . . . OK. . . . Yeah, Sally enjoyed the other night too. Thanks again. OK. . . . Bye." |
| *Lawrence:* | [Steps back into the office.] "What do you think about the Gerald proposal?" |

*Thompson:*  "I don't like it. It doesn't fit with what we've promised Corporate or Hines."

*Lawrence:*  "Yeah, that's what I thought too. What is Jerry going to do about it?"

*Thompson:*  "I haven't talked to him yet. [He turns to the phone and dials.] Let's see if he's in."

This dialogue may seem chaotic to an outsider, but that's only because an outsider does not share the business or organizational knowledge these managers have and does not know Thompson's agenda. That is, an outsider would not know who Potter, Ted, Phyllis, Bill Larson, Sally, Hines, or Jerry are, or what exactly "Chicago," "April numbers," "CD," or the "Gerald proposal" refer to. Nor would an outsider know what role Potter or Hines plays in Thompson's agenda. But to someone with that knowledge, the conversations make sense.

But more important, beyond being "not chaotic," these conversations are in fact amazingly efficient. In less than two minutes Thompson accomplished all of the following.

1. He learned that Mike Potter agreed to help on a particular problem loan. That problem, if not resolved successfully, could have seriously hurt Thompson's plan to increase the division's business in a certain area.

2. He reminded one of his managers to call someone in Chicago in reference to that loan.

3. He found out that the plans for the next week, about that loan, were all set. These included two internal meetings and a talk with the client.

4. He learned that Ted Jenkins was feeling better after an operation. Ted worked for Thompson and was an important part of Thompson's plans for the direction of the division over the next two years.

5 He found out that division income for April was on budget except in one area, which reduced pressures on him to focus on monthly income and to divert attention away from an effort to build revenues in one area.

6. He initiated a meeting with George Masolia to talk about the April figures. Thompson had been considering various future alternatives for the CD product line, which he felt must get on budget to support his overall thrust for the division.

7. He provided some information (as a favor) to Bill Larson, a peer in another part of the bank. Larson had been very helpful to Thompson in the past and was in a position to be very helpful in the future.

8. He initiated a call to Jerry Wilkins, one of his subordinates, to find out his reaction to a proposal from another division that would affect Thompson's division. He was concerned that the proposal could interfere with the division's five-year revenue goals.

In a general sense, John Thompson and most of the other effective GMs I have known are, as one HBR author recently put it, "adept at grasping and taking advantage of each item in the random succession of time and issue fragments that crowd [their] day[s]."[7] This seems to be particularly true for the best performers. And central to their ability to do so are their networks and agendas. The agendas allow the GMs to react in an opportunistic (and highly efficient) way to the flow of events around them, yet knowing that they are doing so within some broader and more rational framework. The networks allow terse (and very efficient) conversations to happen; without them, such short yet meaningful conversations would be impossible. Together, the agenda and networks allow the GMs to achieve the efficiency they need to cope with very demanding jobs in fewer than 60 hours per week (pattern 12), through daily behavior patterns that on the surface can look "unmanagerial."

## WHAT SHOULD TOP MANAGERS DO?

Some of the most important implications of all this include the following:

1. At the start, putting someone in a GM job who does not know the business or the people involved, because he is a successful "professional manager," is probably very risky. Unless the business is easy to learn, it would be very difficult for an individual to learn enough, fast enough, to develop a good agenda. And unless it is a small situation with few people involved, it would be difficult to build a strong network fast enough to implement the agenda.

Especially for large and complex businesses, this condition suggests that "growing" one's own executives should have a high priority. Many companies today say that developing their own executives is important, but in light of the booming executive search business, one has to conclude that either they are not trying very hard or that their efforts simply are not succeeding.

**2.** Management training courses, both in universities and in corporations, probably overemphasize formal tools, unambiguous problems, and situations that deal simplistically with human relationships.

Some of the time-management programs, currently in vogue, are a good example of the problem here. Based on simplistic conceptions about the nature of managerial work, these programs instruct managers to stop letting people and problems "interrupt" their daily work. They often tell potential executives that short and disjointed conversations are ineffective. They advise that one should discipline oneself not to let "irrelevant" people and topics get on one's schedule. In other words, they advise people to behave differently from the effective executives in this study. Seminars on "How to Run Meetings" are probably just as bad.

Another example of inappropriate courses is university-based executive training programs that emphasize formal quantitative tools. These programs are based, at least implicitly, on the assumption that such tools are central to effective performance. All evidence suggests that while they are sometimes relevant, they are hardly central.

**3.** People who are new in general management jobs can probably be gotten up to speed more effectively than is the norm today. Initially, a new GM usually needs to spend considerable time collecting information, establishing relationships, selecting a basic direction for his or her area of responsibilities, and developing a supporting organization. During the first three to six months, demands from superiors to accomplish specific tasks, or to work on pet projects, can often be counterproductive. Indeed, anything that significantly diverts attention away from agenda setting and network building can prove to be counterproductive.

In a more positive sense, those who oversee GMs can probably be most helpful initially if they are sensitive to where the new executive is likely to have problems and help him or her in those areas. Such areas are often quite predictable. For example, if people have spent their careers going up the ladder in one function and have been promoted into the general manager's job in an autonomous division (a common occurrence, especially in manufacturing organizations), they will probably have problems with agenda setting because of a lack of detailed knowledge about the other functions in the division.

On the other hand, if people have spent most of their early careers in professional, staff, or assistant-to jobs and are promoted into a GM's job where they suddenly have responsibility for hundreds or thousands of people (not an unusual occurrence in professional organizations), they will probably have great difficulty at first building a network. They don't have many relationships to begin with and they are not used to spending time developing a large network.

In either case, a GM's boss can be a helpful coach and can arrange activities that foster instead of retard the types of actions the new executive should be taking.

**4.** Finally, the formal planning systems within which many GMs must operate probably hinder effective performance.

A good planning system should help a GM create an intelligent agenda and a strong network that can implement it. That is, it should encourage the GM to think strategically, to consider both the long and short term, and, regardless of the time frame, to take into account financial, product / market, and organizational issues. Furthermore, it should be a flexible tool that the executive can use to help build a network. It should give the GM leeway and options, so that, depending on what kind of environment among subordinates is desired, he or she can use the planning system to help achieve the goals.

Unfortunately, many of the planning systems used by corporations do nothing of the sort. Instead, they impose a rigid "number crunching" requirement on GMs that often does not require much strategic or long-range thinking in agenda setting and which can make network building and maintenance needlessly difficult by creating unnecessary stress among people. Indeed, some systems seem to do nothing but generate paper, often a lot of it, and distract executives from doing those things that are really important.

## BASIS OF THE STUDY

Conducted between 1976 and 1981, this study focused on a group of successful general managers in nine corporations. I examined what their jobs entailed, who they were, where they had come from, how they behaved, and how this all varied in different corporate and industry settings.

The participants all had some profit center and multifunctional responsibility. They were located in cities across the United States. They were involved in a broad range of industries, including banking, consulting, tire and rubber manufacture, TV, mechanical equipment manufacture, newspapers, copiers, investment management, consumer products, and still others. The businesses they were responsible for included some doing only $1 million to $10 million in sales, others in the $10 million to $50 million range, the $50 million to $100 million range, the $100 million to $1 billion range, and some doing

CONTINUED

$1 billion or more. On average, these executives were 47 years old. In 1978, they were paid (on average) about $150,000 (that is, well over $200,000 in 1982 dollars). And all, when selected, were believed to be performing well in their jobs.

Data collection involved three visits to each GM over 6 to 12 months. Each time I interviewed them for at least five hours, often more. I observed their daily routine for about 35 hours, and I interviewed for an hour each the dozen or so key people with whom each worked. The GMs filled out two questionnaires and gave me relevant documents, such as business plans, appointment diaries, and annual reports. From these various sources, I obtained information on the GMs' backgrounds, personalities, jobs, job contexts, behavior, and performance. Because data collection involved considerable effort for each individual, I had to limit the number of GMs selected for study to 15.

I measured the performance of the GMs by combining "hard" and "soft" indexes. The former included measures of revenue and profit growth, both in an absolute sense and compared with plans. The latter included opinions of people who worked with the GMs (including bosses, subordinates, and peers), as well as, when possible, industry analysts. Using this method, I judged most of the GMs to be doing a "very good" job. A few were rated "excellent" and a few "good / fair."

# Notes

## CHAPTER 2
### Choosing Strategies for Change

   1. Niccolò Machiavelli, *The Prince*.
   2. Marvin Bower and C. Lee Walton, Jr., "Gearing a Business to the Future," in *Challenge to Leadership* (New York: The Conference Board, 1973), p. 126.
   3. For recent evidence on the frequency of changes, see Stephen A. Allen, "Organizational Choice and General Influence Networks for Diversified Companies," *Academy of Management Journal* (September 1978): 341.
   4. For example, see Robert A. Luke, Jr., "A Structural Approach to Organizational Change," *Journal of Applied Behavioral Science* (September–October 1973): 611.
   5. For a discussion of power and politics in corporations, see Abraham Zaleznik and Manfred F. R. Kets de Vries, *Power and the Corporate Mind* (Boston: Houghton Mifflin, 1975), Chapter 6; and Robert H. Miles, *Macro Organizational Behavior* (Pacific Palisades, Calif.: Goodyear, 1978), Chapter 4.
   6. See Edgar H. Schein, *Organizational Psychology* (Englewood Cliffs, N.J.: Prentice-Hall, 1965), p. 44.
   7. See Chris Argyris, *Intervention Theory and Method* (Reading, Mass.: Addison-Wesley, 1970), p. 70.
   8. See Paul R. Lawrence, "How to Deal with Resistance to Change," *Harvard Business Review* (May–June 1954): 49; reprinted as HBR Classic, January–February 1969, p. 4.

**9.** For a discussion of resistance that is personality based, see Goodwin Watson, "Resistance to Change," in *The Planning of Change,* eds. Warren G. Bennis, Kenneth F. Benne, and Robert Chin (New York: Holt, Rinehart, and Winston, 1969), p. 489.

**10.** Peter F. Drucker, *The Practice of Management* (New York: Harper and Row, 1954).

**11.** For a general discussion of resistance and reasons for it, see Chapter 3 in Gerald Zaltman and Robert Duncan, *Strategies for Planned Change* (New York: John Wiley, 1977).

**12.** See, for example, Alfred J. Marrow, David F. Bowers, and Stanley E. Seashore, *Management by Participation* (New York: Harper and Row, 1967).

**13.** Zaltman and Duncan, *Strategies for Planned Change,* Chapter 4.

**14.** For an excellent discussion of negotiation, see Gerald I. Nierenberg, *The Art of Negotiating* (Birmingham, Ala.: Cornerstone, 1968).

**15.** See John P. Kotter, "Power, Dependence, and Effective Management," *Harvard Business Review* (July–August 1977): 125.

**16.** Ibid., p. 135.

**17.** See Larry E. Greiner, "Patterns of Organization Change," *Harvard Business Review* (May–June 1967): 119; and Larry E. Greiner and Louis B. Barnes, "Organization Change and Development," in *Organizational Change and Development,* eds. Gene W. Dalton and Paul R. Lawrence (Homewood, Ill.: Irwin, 1970), p. 3.

**18.** For a good discussion of an approach that attempts to minimize resistance, see Renato Tagiuri, "Notes on the Management of Change: Implication of Postulating a Need for Competence," in John P. Kotter, Leonard A. Schlesinger, and Vijay Sathe, *Organization* (Homewood, Ill.: Irwin, 1979).

**19.** Jay W. Lorsch, "Managing Change," in *Organizational Behavior and Administration,* eds. Paul R. Lawrence, Louis B. Barnes, and Jay W. Lorsch (Homewood, Ill.: Irwin, 1976), p. 676.

**20.** Ibid.

**21.** Ibid.

**22.** Michael Beer, *Organization Change and Development: A Systems View* (Pacific Palisades, Calif.: Goodyear, 1980).

## CHAPTER 5

### Power, Dependence, and Effective Management

**1.** Charles A. Reich, *The Greening of America: How the Youth Revolution Is Trying to Make America Liveable* (New York: Random House, 1970).

**2.** See Leonard R. Sayles, *Managerial Behavior: Administration in Complex Organization* (New York: McGraw-Hill, 1964) as well as Rosemary Stewart,

*Managers and Their Jobs* (London: Macmillan, 1967) and *Contrasts in Management* (London: McGraw-Hill, 1976).

**3.** I am talking about the type of inexplicable differences that Henry Mintzberg has found; see his article "The Manager's Job: Folklore and Fact," *Harvard Business Review* (March–April 1990): 163.

**4.** These categories closely resemble the five developed by John R. P. French and Bertram Raven; see "The Base of Social Power," *Group Dynamics: Research and Theory*, Dorwin Cartwright and Alvin Zandler, eds. (New York: Harper & Row, 1968), Chapter 20. Three of the categories are similar to the types of "authority"-based power described by Max Weber in *The Theory of Social and Economic Organization* (New York: Free Press, 1947).

**5.** For an excellent discussion of this method, see Richard E. Neustadt, *Presidential Power* (New York: John Wiley, 1960).

**6.** See Edward C. Banfield, *Political Influence* (New York: Free Press, 1965), Chapter 11.

**7.** See David C. McClelland and David H. Burnham, "Power Is the Great Motivator," *Harvard Business Review* (March–April 1976): 100.

## CHAPTER 7
### What Effective General Managers Really Do

**1.** Such as Sune Carlson, *Executive Behavior: A Study of the Work Load and the Working Methods of Managing Directors* (Stockholm, Sweden: Stromberg, 1951); Thomas Burns, "Management in Action," *Operational Research Quarterly* 8 (1957); Rosemary Stewart, "To Understand the Manager's Job: Consider Demands, Constraints, Choices," *Organizational Dynamics* (Spring 1976): 22; Michael Cohen and James March, *Leadership and Ambiguity* (New York: McGraw-Hill, 1974); R. Dubin and S. L. Spray, "Executive Behavior and Interaction," *Industrial Relations* 3 (1964): 99; and E. Brewer and J. W. C. Tomlinson, "The Manager's Working Day," *Journal of Industrial Economics* 12 (1964): 191.

**2.** See Morgan McCall, Ann Morrison, and Robert Hannan, "Studies of Managerial Work: Results and Methods," Technical Report No. 9 (Greensboro, N.C.: Center for Creative Leadership, 1978). This excellent report summarizes dozens of different studies ranging from Sune Carlson's groundbreaking work in 1951 to recent work by Mintzberg, Stewart, and others.

**3.** See "The Manager's Job: Folklore or Fact," *Harvard Business Review* (July–August 1975): 49.

**4.** Although these patterns are not widely recognized in today's conventional wisdom on management, there is evidence from other studies that GMs and other top managers do use such a process. See, for example, James Brian

Quinn, *Strategies for Change: Logical Incrementalism* (Homewood, Ill: Richard D. Irwin, 1980); Henry Mintzberg, *The Nature of Managerial Work* (New York: Harper & Row, 1973); H. Edward Wrapp, "Good Managers Don't Make Policy Decisions," *Harvard Business Review* (September–October 1967): 91; Charles Lindblom, "The Science of 'Muddling Through,'" *Public Administration Review* 19 (1959): 79; James March and Herbert Simon, *Organizations* (New York: John Wiley, 1958); Chester Barnard, *The Functions of the Executive* (Cambridge: Harvard University Press, 1939); Rosemary Stewart, "Managerial Agendas—Reactive or Proactive," *Organizational Dynamics* (Autumn 1979): 34; Frank Aguilar, *Scanning the Business Environment* (New York: Macmillan, 1967); and Michael McCaskey, "A Contingency Approach to Planning: Planning with Goals and Planning without Goals," *Academy of Management Journal* (June 1974): 91.

5. Although there is not a great deal of supporting evidence elsewhere, some does exist that is consistent with these findings. See, for example, John F. Gabarro, "Socialization at the Top—How CEOs and Their Subordinates Evolve Interpersonal Contacts," *Organizational Dynamics* (Winter 1979): 2; Jeffrey Pfeffer and Jerry Salancik, "Who Gets Power and How They Hold on to It," *Organizational Dynamics* (Winter 1977): 2; my article, "Power, Dependence, and Effective Management," *Harvard Business Review* (July–August 1977): 125; Melville Dalton, *Men Who Manage* (New York: John Wiley, 1959); and Richard Tanner Pascale and Anthony G. Athos, *The Art of Japanese Management* (New York: Simon & Schuster, 1981).

6. Once again, this type of behavior has been recognized and discussed in some management literature, but not in a great deal of it. See recent work by Thomas J. Peters and Jeffrey Pfeffer, in particular. For example, see Thomas J. Peters, "Symbols, Patterns, and Settings: An Optimistic Case for Getting Things Done," *Organizational Dynamics* (Autumn 1978); and Jeffrey Pfeffer, "Management as Symbolic Action," in *Research in Organizational Behavior*, vol. 3, L. L. Cummings and Barry M. Staw, ed. (Greenwich, Conn.: JAI Press, 1980). Also, see M. Andrew Pettigrew, *The Politics of Organizational Decision Making* (London: Tavistock Publications, 1973); and my article, "Power, Dependence, and Effective Management," *Harvard Business Review* (July–August 1977): 125.

7. Thomas J. Peters, "Leadership: Sad Facts and Silver Linings," *Harvard Business Review* (November–December 1979): 164.

# Index

# About the Author

John P. Kotter is the Konosuke Matsushita Professor of Leadership at the Harvard Business School. A graduate of MIT and Harvard, he has been on the Harvard Business School faculty since 1972. In 1981, at the age of 34, he was given tenure and a full professorship at the school, making him one of the youngest people in Harvard's history to be so honored.

From 1968 to the present, Professor Kotter has been a consultant and a public speaker for more than 400 corporations and public agencies. He has also served on the Army Science Board and the boards of AMI Corporate College, McBer, and Scitex America. His many clients include Advanced Micro Devices, AlliedSignal, Allstate Insurance, Aluminum Company of America, American Cyanamid, American Express, Applicon, ARCO, Australian Institute of Management, Avon, Bain, Banc One Corporation, Bank of Ireland, Barclays, Baxter Healthcare, Bristol-Myers Squibb, CIT Group, CNA Insurance, Coca-Cola, Digital Equipment, Dun & Bradstreet, Fireman's Fund, First Union, General Electric, General Mills, General Motors, GTE, Goodrich, Harris Corporation,

Heidrick & Struggles, Hershey, Honeywell, IBM, Johnson & Johnson, Keithley Instruments, Ketchum Communications, Marriott, McDonnell Douglas, Merrill Lynch, Mobil, Monsanto, Motorola, NCR, Neste, New York Life Insurance, KPMG Peat Marwick, PepsiCo, Phillips, Price Waterhouse, RCA, Reebok International, RJR Nabisco, Sara Lee, Scitex, Scott Paper, Shell Oil, Sony, Southwestern Bell, Time, TRW, and Upjohn.

Professor Kotter is the author of several business books, among them *Matsushita Leadership: Lessons from the 20th Century's Most Remarkable Entrepreneur* (1997), *Leading Change* (1996), *The New Rules: How to Succeed in Today's Post-Corporate World* (1995), *Corporate Culture and Performance* (with James L. Heskett, 1992), *A Force for Change: How Leadership Differs from Management* (1990), *The Leadership Factor* (1988), *Power and Influence: Beyond Formal Authority* (1985), and *The General Managers* (1982). He has also created two highly acclaimed executive videos, *Leadership* (1991) and *Corporate Culture* (1993). His books have been printed in more than 50 foreign language editions, and total book sales are approaching 1 million copies. His articles in the *Harvard Business Review* have sold 1.5 million reprints.

The many honors won by Professor Kotter include first place in the Financial Times, Booz-Allen Global Business Book Competition; an Exxon Award for Innovation in Graduate Business School Curriculum Design; a Johnson, Smith & Knisely Award for New Perspectives in Business Leadership; and a McKinsey Award for best *Harvard Business Review* article.

Professor Kotter lives in Cambridge, Massachusetts, and Ashland, New Hampshire, with his wife, Nancy, and children, Caroline and Jonathan.